CW00351793

Making the most of your freezer

a Consumer Publication

Consumers' Association
publishers of **Which?**
14 Buckingham Street
London WC2N 6DS

a Consumer Publication

edited by   Edith Rudinger

published by   Consumers' Association
publishers of **Which?**

Consumer Publications
are available from
Consumers' Association
and from booksellers.
Details are given at
the end of this book.

© Consumers' Association October 1982

ISBN 0 85202 235 Z
and 0 340 28750 0

 Printed in Great Britain by
Page Bros (Norwich) Ltd

Contents

Should you buy a freezer?

Not so long ago, freezers were a rarity in this country. Nowadays, many people consider a freezer to be a necessity; nearly half of all households possess one.

Not everyone should necessarily buy one. Although financial savings can be made by buying food in bulk and by freezing garden produce, these do not always offset the cost. Freezers cost money to buy; they cost money to run by increasing the electricity bill and because food must be specially packed, and the packaging materials also cost money.

So, if money is tight, the local shops are cheap and you have the time and energy to shop frequently, you may well decide a freezer is not for you.

advantages of owning a freezer

A lot of food can be stored in a freezer. This means that you can buy in bulk and this is usually cheaper. For instance, bulk-buying vegetables and fruit when they are at their lowest price, is an economy. Bulk-buying also means fewer trips to the shops, which means less petrol or fewer bus fares. It also means that instead of always popping to the nearest shop, a journey to a cheaper one becomes worthwhile.

But the greatest savings are for people who are keen gardeners (or have friends and neighbours who are). Then instead of letting raspberries go bad, or throwing away beans when everyone else has them and you cannot face beans for dinner again, you can freeze them. A freezer ensures that each season's glut is kept safe until you choose to eat what you have frozen.

Fewer shopping trips also save time and energy. The working wife does not need to rush down to the shop, frantically snatching a sandwich in the lunch hour. For an old or infirm person, a freezer can be a boon: no need to go shopping if the weather is bad; if you do not have the energy to walk to the shop one day, there is always a meal in the freezer. Sons and daughters with aged parents can prepare an extra portion while cooking at home, freeze it and take it along to keep in mum's freezer so that she can have a substantial meal even if she cannot make the effort, or be bothered, to cook for herself.

Preparing and cooking a meal can be a time-consuming chore, so the motto can be: eat one – freeze two. Prepare and cook when you have the time and inclination, and use the extra portions later. You save gas or electricity by cooking a lot at once (and have only one lot to wash up), if you make it a rule to fill up the oven whenever you use it for baking or roasting. And do not forget that leftovers can often be frozen and not thrown away.

There is also a feeling of luxury about owning a freezer. Cauliflower or beans? peas or sweetcorn? cabbage or broccoli? or any other of the vegetables stored away – the choice is yours, and with a freezer the choice is wide. Or what about coq au vin, prepared for visitors and a couple of extra portions put away a few months ago? With a freezer unexpected guests are no longer an embarrassment because an extra portion is always there. (But remember that some things take a long time to thaw, unless you can use a microwave oven.)

Where to put your freezer

Having decided that a freezer is for you, an important decision is where to put it because this could have a bearing on what type you buy.

The three basic types of freezer are chest freezers (the big white boxes with a hinged lid on the top), upright freezers (which open like a cupboard) and fridge-freezers (essentially upright freezers with a refrigerator, underneath, on top, or, with some newer models, side by side).

Upright freezers are between 50 cm and 60 cm (19¾ in and 23¾ in) wide and 60 cm to 65 cm (23¾ in to 25½ in) deep. Most models also need a 50 mm (about 2 in) gap at the back to allow the warm air to escape and a couple of inches above, for ventilation. On some, you must allow a few extra inches on the width so that you can open the door. This is particularly important for an upright freezer or fridge-freezer with drawers or baskets if you want to place it in a corner. Handles stick out and sometimes you need to open the door more than 90° to get the baskets out. Check before you buy. Some models are designed to go on top of a work surface, some to go under a work surface (85 cm, 33½ in high) and some beside work surfaces (over 85 cm, 33½ in high). Fridge-freezers are taller than the work surfaces (up to 2 metres, 6 ft 6 in) and are best placed at the end of a run of cupboards or other equipment.

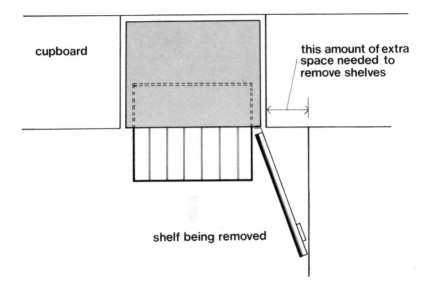

cupboard

this amount of extra
space needed to
remove shelves

shelf being removed

Chest freezers are generally between 70 cm (27½ in) and 180 cm (6 ft) wide and about 65 cm (25½ in) deep. The height is usually between 85 cm (33½ in) and 95 cm (37½ in). You will need to allow an extra 70 cm (27½ in) or so for opening the lid. The overall height needed is therefore about 155 cm to 165 cm (5 ft to 5 ft 5 in). (Beware of overhead cupboards which would prevent you opening the lid fully or on which you might bang your hand as you lift the lid.)

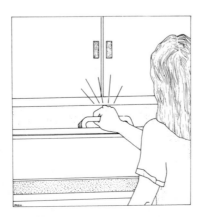

in the kitchen?

This is one obvious, convenient place. But a kitchen tends to be a warm place, particularly when the cooker is in use, and if it houses the central heating boiler, there is an extra source of heat. Remember, the warmer the temperature around the freezer, the more it will cost to run.

Since a freezer operates as a small heater – the heat it extracts from the storage chamber being ejected into the kitchen – in winter it is really costing nothing to run inasmuch as it is contributing to the overall heating of the house. In summer, the opposite applies.

There must be plently of room above the freezer to allow the warm air to escape, particularly if there are cupboards close on each side. About 15 in (40 cm) between the top and a wall cupboard is a reasonable amount; a couple of inches at the top is the very minimum. If you cannot have much space above, leave more at the sides.

Some people want to put a small freezer under a work surface or, for neatness, squash their freezer (or refrigerator) between two cupboards, leaving no gaps at the top either. This is bad: warm air cannot escape, the freezer (or refrigerator) has to work harder and uses more electricity to keep the temperature inside low.

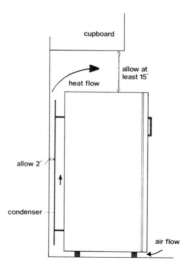

In addition to space at the top, there should also be space at the bottom, so that cool air can go in. Some freezers have virtually no gap between the bottom and the floor and if this is so, you must leave a space at the side and not put cupboards tight up against the side of the freezer.

If you want to put a freezer in a built-in kitchen, do not just build in an ordinary one, but buy a model designed to be built-in. Or try putting the freezer at the end of a run, or buy one that fits under the work surface – but remember to allow space for the warm air to escape, preferably by having a couple of inches to spare at the top.

Kitchens are often too small for all the different appliances used today. Since a freezer needs only a supply of electricity, unlike dishwashers and washing machines which need a water supply and drainage, it may make sense to move the freezer out of the kitchen altogether. Choosing another place may also mean a larger freezer can be bought.

in the garage or outhouse?

Both these places have one important advantage: since they are not heated, the temperature around the freezer is much lower and therefore the freezer costs less to run. In a lower temperature, a freezer has less work to do keeping the inside cold, so it is also less likely to go wrong than one that has to work harder.

But there are disadvantages; the first is inconvenience. If the garage is attached to your house and there is a direct connection to the kitchen, there is no hardship, but if the garage is at the bottom of the garden, putting food in or taking food out means a trudge (shoes and coat on and, more often than not in our climate, getting wet). So it may also mean that you do not bother to make the effort, and the freezer would not be used to its full advantage. A large freezer in the garage for long-term storage, and a fridge-freezer in the kitchen to take the next few days' supplies, may be the answer.

Also, if anything should go wrong with the freezer, because it is out of sight it may be a long time before you notice that something is amiss.

Another disadvantage is dampness. Garages and outhouses are usually very damp places and, like your car, freezers can rust. A coat of silicone polish on the surface will help prevent the freezer rusting. Keep an eye on it, particularly at the back, and treat any rust as soon as it appears. Preventing rust is better than curing it, so allow plenty of air circulation within the garage, particularly if you sometimes put a wet car in there. Keep a window open (if this presents a security risk, put bars across the window).

Keep your freezer off the ground by placing some bricks under the feet. But a freezer is very heavy when full, so you would need engineering bricks to avoid the danger of the bricks fracturing. Or you may be able to use four thick off-cuts of wood. Make sure that the freezer is standing level and firm.

There is also the question of security: a freezer in a garage or outhouse can be burgled. So, the freezer should have a secure lock fastening.

Obviously, there must be an electricity supply to the garage or outhouse. You are not allowed to extend a ring circuit to a separate building. If you want to provide a supply, it has to be a separate circuit with its own fuse at the fuse box (consumer unit) and a second isolating switch and fuse in the other building. There are regulations governing the sort of cable to use, and how to use it.

in the pantry? under the stairs?

There are often spare corners which can be utilised for a freezer. But if a freezer is to keep the food inside cold, it must remove heat and must get rid of this excess heat. (This is why the instructions enclosed with your freezer tell you to allow room for air circulation.) If the pantry or the space under the stairs is enclosed and the heat generated by the freezer cannot escape, the freezer will cost more to run and there is a greater chance of it going wrong.

If there is a utility room or a laundry room in your house, this would be a good place for the freezer. But keep it well away from heat-creating appliances such as a tumble dryer or the central heating boiler.

in the dining room?

If you feel a large white box in the dining room may do little to enhance the decor, consider one in brown, red or cream. Colours are becoming popular and some manufacturers are extending their range. Also, freezers with removable decor panels are available. Or you could furnish the room with built-in units which can hide an upright freezer completely.

A freezer should not stand on a pile carpet which might interfere with air circulation from below. Also, defrosting may be more tedious if you have to take care not to stain the carpet.

Although the noise from a freezer is unlikely to disturb you in the kitchen, it may be annoying in the dining room.

upstairs?

A spare bedroom can house a freezer. But a freezer should not be tilted more than 30° from the vertical at most, so take a careful look at the stairs first – it may be difficult or impossible to get a freezer upstairs if the stairs are not in a straight flight. And remember that freezers are heavy when full, so check that the floor is strong enough to take the weight. Chest freezers spread the load more than uprights. Try and place the freezer across the joists so as to spread the load. (Joists run at right angles to the floor boards.)

in the conservatory?

Conservatories are supposed to be sun-traps, so on the whole putting the freezer there is not a good idea. Even when the air temperature is quite low, the surface of the freezer could get very warm in the sun. Not only does this mean higher electricity bills but, during the summer, the freezer may not be able to cope and the inside of the freezer may become warmer than it should be. You may not notice the difference (unless the freezer has a temperature indicator on the outside), because everything is still frozen solid. However, the storage life of the food inside is drastically shortened. A frozen chicken, for example, will keep for 12 months at −18°C, about a month at −12°C and less than a week at −6°C.

points to remember

Wherever you place your freezer
- avoid having the sun shining on the freezer. This may mean choosing a slightly different position or it may mean fitting a venetian blind to the window

- avoid placing the freezer next to a source of heat, such as a cooker or boiler. If it is inevitable, leave as much space as possible between the two – a gap of at least an inch (about 2½ cm)

- allow plenty of space around the freezer – particularly at the back. Most upright freezers and fridge-freezers and some chest freezers have a black grille at the back known as a static condenser. This is where the freezer loses its excess heat, and room should be left for the warm air to escape. As a guide, leave a couple of inches (about 5 cm) between the wall and the back. Make sure that the gap is not just between the wall and the back edge of the top: it should be between the (perhaps hidden) condenser, lower down, and the wall.

If the freezer has a tendency to slide backwards (many of them have wheels to help move them) put a wedge at the back to maintain the space.

Several types of chest freezer do not have a static condenser but a skin condenser, and lose heat over the outside surface of the freezer. These need about an inch (2½ cm) to be left all around. For a freezer with a static condenser, space at the side is less important.

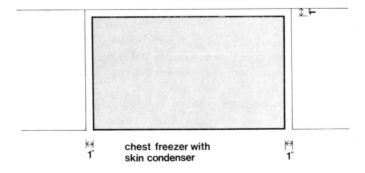

chest freezer with
skin condenser
1″   1″

To get the baskets out of some upright freezers and fridge-freezers, the door has to be open more than 90°. This means that the hinge side cannot go close up to a wall. (It can, however, go close up to a cupboard.)

the advantages of the different types

The advantages of a chest freezer are:
- cheaper to buy
- cheaper to run
- large items are easier to fit in
- less fiddly to clean
- stays cold longer during a power failure.

The advantages of an upright freezer are:
- takes up less floor space
- easier to keep contents organised
- easier to get at things you want.

The advantages of a fridge-freezer are the same as those for upright freezers. Since it combines a refrigerator and a freezer, it takes up even less (valuable) kitchen space.

So, choose a fridge-freezer if space is a problem, choose an upright freezer for convenience and choose a chest freezer for economy.

chest freezers – things to look for

If you are going to keep your freezer in a garage or outhouse, choose a freezer with a skin condenser (that is, one that does not have a large black panel at the back). Condensation on the outer surface of the freezer can start problems of rusting, but freezers with skin condensers lose their heat from pipes buried just beneath the outer surface, so that the outer surface is slightly warm to touch and this will help to prevent condensation. A freezer with a skin condenser tends to be a little more expensive, but worth considering for putting in a garage or outhouse.

base
It is worth checking that the material of the underneath of the freezer is solid. Many of the cheaper models have only cardboard or foil

covering the insulation. If this gets damaged, moisture can get into the insulation. Look – that is, feel with your fingers – for a freezer with a solid (metal) base, particularly if your are going to keep it in a garage or outhouse.

insulation
Usually, the insulation is approximately 50 mm (2 in) thick. There are now freezers with thicker insulation. This makes them smaller inside, but they are slightly cheaper to run.

counterbalanced lid
Most chest freezers have a lid which will stay in position until almost closed, but there are some in which the lid falls under its own weight unless it is fully open. A freezer lid is heavy and can bruise fingers if they are inadvertently left in the way. Avoid a freezer without a counterbalanced lid, particularly if there are small children around you – they often have the habit of putting their hands over the edge of an open freezer, trying to look inside. A heavy lid falling on small fingers can have serious consequences. (A large hook in the wall behind, to come over the lid when opened, eliminates the risk of the lid falling on fingers.)

If you are on the short side, or arthritic, check (before you buy) that you can reach down to the bottom at the back – not only for taking out items, but also for mopping up when defrosting. It is a long way down.

lock
If your freezer is going to be in a garage or outhouse, get one with a lock. While you may be able to identify granny's ring if it is stolen, a leg of lamb that was in your freezer is less distinctive. Also, a lock deters teenagers from raiding the freezer and prevents unsupervised small children from lifting the lid and possibly falling in.

drain hole
Choose a freezer with a drainage hole, if you do not want the chore of bailing out the water after the freezer has defrosted. Check that it is in a convenient place, so that you can put a basin there and remove it when full.

position of controls
Most chest freezers have the controls at the bottom corner, which is not very convenient if you find it difficult to bend down, but is ideal

for small children who will adore playing with the pretty lights. On some models there is a plastic cover which slides over the fast-freeze switch and the on-off switch. This makes it more difficult to knock the switch accidentally, but not impossible for an inquisitive child to turn off your freezer.

upright freezers – things to look for

If you want to freeze or store a large item, you could have problems with an upright freezer.

shelves and baskets
If there are baskets (which are, in fact, drawers), they take up some storage space, which is a disadvantage. But when it comes to defrosting, they have the advantage that you can take them out with the food inside and keep the food in the basket (covered for insulation).

At the top of a tall freezer, shelves are more convenient than drawers which you may find difficult to reach into. Conversely, at the bottom pull-out drawers or baskets are more convenient than shelves. Drawers or shelf-fronts which have an open grille allow you to see what is inside, which can be very useful. Check whether the shelves and/or baskets are removable and check that any baskets that are provided are deep enough and robust enough not to bend under the weight of one large item.

Also check that there are no large gaps between the rows. If there are, when the baskets are full and you remove one, packets tend to fall off down the back. This is irritating and might stop you using your freezer to full advantage.

Baskets or drawers should have stops so that you cannot pull them out to beyond about halfway without their stopping. It should not be possible to replace the drawer or basket incorrectly so that the stop would not work. Check, too, that the baskets or drawers will not tip up when in this position.

controls
An upright freezer can have the controls in a variety of places. If they are at the top, make sure you can reach them. If they are at the bottom, small children may intefere with them when playing. Sometimes the controls are inside the freezer, which is slightly less convenient but safer from persistent knob twiddlers.

convenience

Consider whether the freezer will be easy to clean: are the shelves or baskets removable, leaving just six plain surfaces to be wiped? Are there any places where dirt can collect and that cannot be reached with a cloth – for instance, refrigerated shelves which have a double layer of wires: crumbs which lodge there can be very difficult to get off. Run you hand gently over all surfaces and into all little nooks and crannies, feeling for sharp edges and corners on which you might bang or cut your hand while cleaning.

fridge-freezers – things to look for

A fridge-freezer is a combination of a refrigerator and an upright freezer, in one unit. This saves on floor space. There are two types: those where the two parts are controlled independently and have two separate compressors (the top is usually a medium-sized refrigerator and the lower part the freezer), and those where the two – fridge and freezer – are run by one single compressor. With this type, the freezer is generally smaller and on top of the refrigerator. This type is also sometimes called a double door fridge. The doors are one above the other, not side by side.

Check that the refrigerator section has all the features you want; you are likely to use the refrigerator more frequently than the freezer, so this may be the most important consideration.

Make sure that the freezer and refrigerator are in the right proportion to your needs. There are some models on the market in which the fridge and the freezer are the same size, either one above the other, or side by side.

The single-compressor type is cheaper to buy, but there is no separate control of the temperture in the freezer, so that the freezer may become too warm if the kitchen gets cold (for example, at night if you do not heat it). The refrigerator is cold enough for its thermostat setting, so that the compressor does not switch on even though it should do so for the freezer part. On the other hand, if you freeze down a lot of food in the freezer part, for which the compressor has to be on continuously, the refrigerator part can get too cold.

So, if you intend keeping a fridge-freezer in a place that gets colder than, say 16°C (61°F), you should buy a two-compressor type, even though it is more expensive.

It is possible to buy separately a freezer and refrigerator that can be stacked on top of each other. The refrigerator may be a larder fridge, that is, one without a frozen food compartment.

other points to note

Whatever type of freezer you decide on, there are several features which may be important to you.

Some freezers have adjustable feet, which is useful if the floor is uneven. Some have rollers which makes it easy to pull out for cleaning behind it.

interior lights

If your freezer is in a place where light is poor, an interior light which comes on every time the door or lid is opened could be very useful. It also provides a useful check that the freezer is still connected to the electricity supply (and that, for instance, nobody has unplugged it by accident). For this reason there is often a mains-on light, which is lit whenever the freezer is connected to the mains whether the compressor is running or not.

control and warning lights

There are usually two lights on most freezers, but their use is not standardised, so it can be confusing if you are used to a freezer with a different set of light signals.

The most common combination is a mains-on light, which is always on when the freezer is on, and a temperature-warning light, which switches itself on only when the temperature is too high inside the freezer – for instance, when the freezer is newly switched on, or when a lot of new food is being frozen-down, or because you have left the door open too long, or maybe because there is something wrong with the freezer.

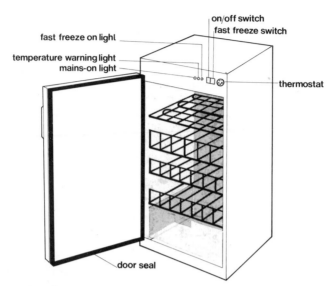

This warning light then switches itself off when the temperature is again right. The disadvantage is that the light will not come on if the mains supply has been switched off or there is a power failure or power cut.

On some freezers there is a combined light which comes on when the temperature inside the freezer is low enough, and switches itself off when the temperature is too warm (or when there is no electricity coming through to the freezer).

Or there may be a temperature warning light which starts winking when the temperature is getting too high inside the freezer.

An audible alarm which sounds when the temperature gets too high is available with some freezers.

Most freezers – but not fridge-freezers with only one compressor – have an indicator light which comes on when the fast-freeze is switched on. The fast-freeze switch usually bypasses the thermostat so that the compressor runs continuously and goes on running.

thermostat control

The temperature inside the freezer is controlled by the thermostat. It does this by switching the compressor on when the temperature inside rises a little, and off when the temperature has dropped sufficiently.

All freezers have thermostats. Some thermostats are pre-set and need a service engineer to make any further adjustments. Other thermostats are adjustable by you and a knob is provided, marked with numbers or a gradually widening band. With some, the knob can be turned by hand but often, to prevent accidents, the knob has a slot, into which a coin has to be inserted to turn it. This is particularly useful if someone in your family is a knob-twiddler.

– thermostat settings
Usually 0 is off, and the settings are indicated in figures, symbols or words.

figures: 1 is the least cold and 7 (or whatever is the highest figure), the coldest

symbols: a band; the thicker, the colder

words: min, normal, max, where min is the least cold and max the coldest.

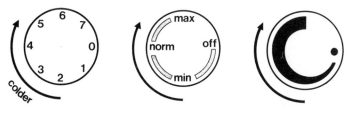

position of controls

The on/off switch, fast-freeze switch, thermostat and the lights can be in a number of places on the freezer. They should be easy to use and convenient to get at but not in a position where they can be accidentally knocked. Too near the floor would be convenient for small children who like playing switching the lights on and off.

amount that can be frozen in 24 hours

The figures quoted by the manufacturer (and given on the rating plate of the freezer) are found by laboratory tests in which a food substitute is used. This substitute behaves like lean beef, and the weight which can be frozen in 24 hours is reasonably accurate for beef. You can freeze more of things like bread which contain only small amounts of water, and less of things like carrots which contain a lot more.

How a freezer works

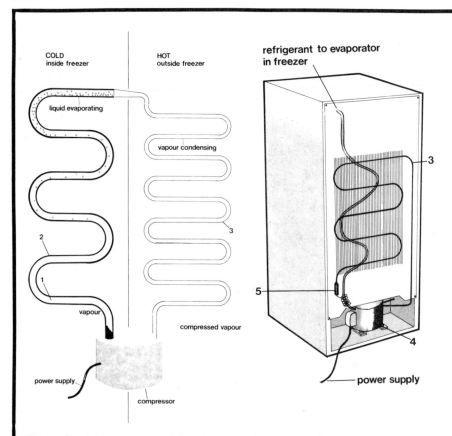

When liquid evaporates (that is, turns into vapour) it removes heat from its surrounding area and cools it. The more quickly it evaporates, the faster heat is removed.

In a freezer, a special liquid (the refrigerant) evaporates very quickly as it passes through a series of tubes (the evaporator) which are placed in the walls or shelves inside the freezer. Continuity is maintained by the action of an electrical pump (the compressor) turning the vapour back into a liquid. When a vapour is turned back into a liquid it gives out heat; the heat is lost in a series of tubes (the condenser) placed outside the freezer cabinet.

Refrigerant: a liquid which evaporates very easily; in doing so, it
1 absorbs heat from the surrounding area (the metal through which it flows), cooling it.

Evaporator: a series of metal tubes in which the refrigerant evaporates;
2 in an upright freezer may be set into the metal shelves; in a chest freezer, the tubes may be buried behind the inner walls of the chest (can be seen outlined by the first traces of frost when the freezer is switched on again after defrosting).

Condenser: a long snake-shaped tube in which the refrigerant turns
3 from vapour to liquid and in doing so gives out heat which is lost to the surrounding air.

Attached to the tube, usually at the back of the freezer may be metal fins or rods to increase the surface area through which heat is lost (*static condenser*).

On some freezers the loss of heat from the fins is helped by a fan blowing air across it (*fan condenser*). The condenser can then be smaller than the more familiar static condenser. Fan condensers are noisier, particularly if the fan is on all the time rather than switched on and off in tandem with the pump, but are slightly better for use where the air temperatures are high.

In chest freezers, the condenser may be buried beneath the outer layer of the freezer wall (*skin condenser*). The location of the buried pipes can be felt where the outside is warm to the touch.

Compressor: an electrically driven pump bolted to the back or side of
4 the freezer; a small layer of rubber cushions the vibration.

Drier unit: contains moisture-absorbing crystals; generally only
5 comes into play once in a freezer's life. Any moisture contained in the refrigerant is removed by the drier unit when the freezer is switched on the very first time.

What size?

Fridge-freezers can have a freezing compartment as small as 1 cu ft (28 litres); the largest freezing compartment of a fridge-freezer is unlikely to be larger than 7 cu ft (198 litres). Upright freezers are usually between 2 cu ft (57 litres) and 15 cu ft (425 litres). Chest freezers vary from 4 cu ft (113 litres) to 23 cu ft (650 litres).

The capacity of a freezer is quoted in cubic feet (cu ft) or litres (l). As a very rough guide, to convert litres into cubic feet, divide by 30 (1 cu ft = 28.3 litres, 1 litre = 0·035 cu ft).

The figure quoted by the manufacturer is generally the gross volume. This can be a little misleading because it includes all the cavities, rounded corners and space above any load line where food cannot or should not be stored. Sometimes the net volume is quoted, which subtracts all these places. There is usually only a small difference between gross and net volumes of chest freezers, but a lot of storage space can be lost in upright freezers, particularly if the baskets are a little undersized.

The size of the freezer you buy is likely to depend to some extent on the space you have, and also on the number of mouths to feed.

As a basic rule of thumb, allow 2 cu ft per person plus an extra 2 cu ft. This means that for a family of four, a 10 cu ft freezer is needed – which is an upright freezer just over 5 ft (150 cm) tall, or a chest freezer about 3 ft 6 in (about 110 cm) wide. For large eaters you should allow more, for those with small appetites, less. If someone in the family is a keen gardener, allow more. Also, allow more to store the results of intensive baking sessions if the family is keen on home-made cakes and scones.

The amount of storage space you need in the freezer obviously depends on
- the number of people you cook for in your household
- how many meals you actually prepare
- how often you entertain guests to a meal, and how many guests
- the variety of foods your family wants to eat
- how often you shop and how convenient the shops are.

how much food can be stored?

One litre of water occupies a volume of a 10 cm cube (approximately a 4 in cube) and weighs 1 kg (just over 2 lb). One kg of meat will occupy about the same volume. But the same weight of carrots will occupy nearly twice as much space and white bread about seven times as much space.

Many people buy a freezer that is too small. Empty, sitting in a shop, a freezer looks like a cavernous hold and you may think 'we could never eat through that much food!' – but you could.

the cost of running it

The bigger the freezer, the more electricity it uses – but it uses it only to make the compressor pump the refrigerant around. If the freezer – that is, the pump – were working continuously for 24 hours a day (which it hardly ever is), it would use up about as much electricity as if you left one 100 watt electric light bulb switched on all day.

Electricity consumption at different room temperatures

temperature in the area surrounding the freezer °C	electricity consumption as a percentage of normal ('100') level %
+32 (kitchen, very hot)	145
+25 (kitchen, normal)	100
+20 (usual room temp)	81
+15 (outhouse, cool)	63

As the table shows, the surrounding temperature greatly affects electricity consumption. If the freezer is put in the kitchen, you should make sure that it is not placed next to the cooker or oven, nor by a window in direct sunlight as this would increase the running costs.

There are many more freezers on the market than you will find locally. Major manufacturers and distributors include:

AEG   AEG Telefunken (UK) Ltd,
217 Bath Road,
Slough,
Berks SL1 4AW
Tel: 0753 872101

ADMIRAL   Trembath Refrigeration Ltd,
414 Purley Way,
Croydon,
Surrey
Tel: 01-651 3020

BAUKNECHT   Beekay Bauknecht Ltd,
6 Priorswood Place,
East Pimbo,
Skelmersdale,
Lancs WN8 9QS
Tel: 0695 21331

BEJAM   Bejam Group Ltd,
1 Garland Road,
Honeypot Lane,
Stanmore
Middx HA7 1LE
Tel: 01-952 8311

BERKLEY   Currys Ltd,
46–50 Uxbridge Road,
Ealing,
London W5 2SU
Tel: 01-567 6611

BOSCH   Robert Bosch Ltd,
Rhodes Way,
Radlett Road,
Watford,
Herts WD2 4LB
Tel: 0923 44233

CANDY   Candy Ltd,
Armour House,
Bridge Street,
Guildford,
Surrey GU1 4SB
Tel: 0483 576031

CARAVELL   Caravell Appliances,
21–23 St. Leonards Lane,
Edinburgh EH8 9SH
Tel: 031-668 2756

CARLTON   Currys Ltd,
46–50 Uxbridge Road,
Ealing,
London W5 2SU
Tel: 01-567 6611

COLSTON   Colston Domestic Appliances Ltd,
Colston House,
London Road,
High Wycombe,
Bucks HP11 1BQ
Tel: 0494 33499

CO-OP   contact your local Co-op

CORDON BLEU   Cordon Bleu Freezer Food Centres Ltd,
St Christopher House,
217 Wellington Road South,
Stockport,
Ches FK2 6QW
Tel: 061-480 4919

DKK   USC Consumer Products (UK Agents for DKK)
Electrical Division,
Sterling House,
Heddon Street,
London W1R 8BP
Tel: 01-734 7080

ELECTRA   Electricity Council,
30 Millbank
London SW1
Tel: 01-834 2333

ELECTROLUX   Electrolux Ltd,
Oakley Road,
Luton,
Beds LO4 9QW
Tel: 0582 53255

FAGOR   Fagor UK,
4 Rangemoor Road,
Tottenham,
London N15
Tel: 01-801 7212

FRIGIDAIRE   Frigidaire Marketing, Unit R,
Gildersome Spur, Distribution Centre,
Morley,
Leeds LS27 7JZ
Tel: 0532 520311/531166

GRAM Gram Refrigeration (GB) Ltd,
95 Cray Avenue,
Orpington,
Kent BR5 3PZ
Tel: 0689 36311

HIRUNDO Indesit House,
25A Progress Way,
Croydon CR0 4XD
Tel: 01-680 8242

HOOVER Hoover Ltd,
20 Wordsworth Road,
Perivale,
Greenford,
Middx UB6 7JY
Tel: 01-997 3311

HOTPOINT Hotpoint Ltd,
Celta Road,
Peterborough PE2 9JB
Tel: 0733 68989

HUSQVARNA Husqvarna Ltd,
PO Box 10,
Oakley Road,
Luton,
Beds LU4 9QW
Tel: 0582 53255

IGNIS Currys Ltd,
46–50 Uxbridge Road,
Ealing,
London W5 2SU
Tel: 01-567 6611

INDESIT Indesit Ltd,
Indesit House,
25A Progress Way,
Croydon CR0 4XD
Tel: 01-680 8242

KELVINATOR Kelco Ltd,
Newchester Road,
Bromborough,
Ches L62 3PE
Tel: 051-334 2781

LEC Lec Refrigeration Ltd,
Bognor Regis,
West Sussex PO22 9NQ
Tel: 0243 863161

MIELE Miele Co Ltd,
Fairacres,
Marcham Road,
Abingdon,
Oxon OX14 1TW
Tel: 0235 28585

NEFF Neff (UK) Ltd,
The Quadrangle,
Westmount Centre,
Uxbridge Road,
Hayes,
Middx UB4 0HD
Tel: 01-848 3711

NORFROST Norfrost Ltd,
Murray Field,
Castletown,
Caithness KW14 8TY
Tel: 084 782 333

NOVUM Novum (Overseas) Ltd,
Kilmore Road,
Artane,
Dublin 5
Tel: 0001 473266

OCEAN Jaimex Marketing Consultants,
2 Crampton Road,
London SE20
Tel: 01-778 0154

OSBY Albec Electrical Ltd,
43C Milton Trading Estate,
Abingdon,
Oxon OX14 4SH
Tel: 0235 831985

PHILCO Philco (GB) Ltd,
458 Heather Park Drive,
Wembley,
Middx HA0 1SR
Tel: 01-902 9626

PHILIPS Philips Electrical Ltd,
Major Appliances Division,
Lightcliff Factory,
Hipperholme,
Halifax,
W Yorks HX3 8DE
Tel: 0422 203511

PILOT   Rumbelows Ltd,
Trinity House,
Trinity Lane,
Waltham Cross,
Herts EN8 7EQ
Tel: 0992 28931

POLAR KING   Comet
POLAR QUEEN   King Charles House,
George Street,
Hull HU1 3AU
Tel: 0482 20681

SCANDINOVA   Vestfrost,
Tangley House,
Aston Rowant,
Oxon OX9 5SN
Tel: 0844 52906

SIBIR   Sibir Refrigeration Ltd,
Unit 16,
Fairview Estate,
Church St,
Dunstable,
Beds NU5 4HU
Tel: 0582 66915
(only gas fridge-freezer, Gascold)

SKANDILUXE   Interset Ltd,
Telford Road,
Basingstoke RG21 2UY
Tel: 0256 62881

SOVEREIGN   Trident,
Telefusion Ltd,
Telefusion House,
Preston New Road,
Blackpool FY4 4QT
Tel: 0253 66111

TRICITY   Thorn-EMI Domestic Appliances (Electrical) Ltd,
New Lane,
Havant,
Hants PO9 2NH
Tel: 0705 486400

VESTFROST   Anton Refrigeration Services Ltd,
Anton Trading Estate,
Andover,
Hants SP10 2NG
Tel: 0264 61361

WOODS   Trembath Refrigeration Ltd,
414 Purley Way,
Croydon,
Surrey
Tel: 01-651 3020

ZANUSSI   IAZ International (UK) Ltd,
Zanussi House,
82 Caversham Road,
Reading RG1 8DA
Tel: 0734 470011

ZEROWATT   Zerowatt Spa,
27A Maidstone Road,
Chatham,
Kent ME4 6DD
Tel: 0634 41204

Before buying

Read the relevant *Which?* reports and try and look at advertising leaflets for as many freezers as possible. If these leaflets are not readily available in the shops, you might try your local electricity board showroom, or you may have to write or phone the various companies direct. If you do, ask also where there are stockists near you.

With the help of leaflets and literature and a list of your requirements, you can make up a short-list of suitable models. Go and look at some of these in your local stores and check on the things the manufacturers do not tell you, such as ease of cleaning, or reaching to the bottom of a chest freezer.

prices

The next step is to find out the price so that you can buy your freezer where you can get it the cheapest. This may be your local electricity board shop, it may be one of a chain of electrical dealers, a department store during a sale, or a small local firm. It may be one of the large cut-price warehouses. Phoning, in the afternoon, can often be cheaper than visiting all the places personally. Electrical chain stores (such as Currys or Rumbelows), the Co-op, your local electricity board, some discount stores (such as Comet and Trident) and freezer food centres (such as Bejam and Cordon Bleu), do not make their own freezers but buy them from the manufacturer and sell them under their own brand name, sometimes significantly cheaper. Look in recent *Which?* reports for 'similar models'.

Not all shops will be able to obtain the model you want, so do ask for prices of alternative models. A slightly larger or last-year's model may in fact be a better buy.

In checking prices, ask whether delivery is included. If it is extra, you may find that what looks like a bargain is not so cheap after all. Much damage can be done when moving a freezer. If the shop delivers the freezer and installs it and it then does not work, they cannot claim it is your responsibility: on the contrary, they will have to compensate you.

guarantees and insurance

When buying a new freezer, check what guarantee you are getting. Some manufacturers offer only a one-year guarantee, but many now offer a 5-year one, which could be worth having.

Various insurance companies offer freezer insurance either as a separate policy, or as an extension to a householder's contents policy. If you get freezer contents insurance as an extension to your house contents policy or included in it, the maximum cover may be limited (to perhaps £100 which would be inadequate if you have a lot of meat or other expensive food in a large freezer). If the standard amount of cover offered by your policy is too low, ask whether the company will give you more cover and what the premium would be.

But before you take out this or any other insurance for your freezer, weigh up whether the amount of food you keep makes the premium worthwhile – and bear in mind the circumstances in which you would not be covered. Some extras that are offered with the policy may seem attractive (such as the free loan of a replacement freezer if yours cannot be mended on the spot). As with all other types of insurance, the cover varies. Some points to watch out for are
– does it cover just the contents or the cabinet itself?
– does it cover the cost of repair of the cabinet?
– does it cover theft of contents?
– does it cover the results of accidents, such as switching the freezer off by mistake?
– does it cover loss when the loss is due to power cuts caused by industrial action?
– does the insurance have to be taken out for a fixed period, such as 5 years?
– does the premium increase after the first two or three years?

other things to buy

All sorts of other things are for sale to the freezer owner, some more important than others.

freezer thermometer

If you are going to adjust your thermostat yourself, a thermometer is essential for doing this correctly. And it is always useful to have a freezer thermometer to check that your freezer is functioning correctly, it may provide an early warning that things are going wrong. It is important to check the temperature in different parts of the freezer, particularly the top of an upright or the top basket in a chest freezer.

freezer baskets

A chest freezer can be made more convenient if the inside is divided up with baskets. Extra baskets for whatever make of freezer can be bought for a few pounds each from specialist outlets such as Hamster Baskets, Much Marcle, Herefordshire (send s.a.e. for a brochure).

blanching basket

This may be useful, particularly if you are going to freeze a lot of vegetables and have no suitable alternative such as a chip-pan basket. Make sure that the basket fits inside your (largest) saucepan – one that holds about 8 pints (4½ litres).

packaging material

The food you freeze will require packaging. Some of the things you use for this are things that you probably have anyway – aluminium foil, plastic boxes, foil dishes, polythene bags. But not all polythene is suitable: it must be thicker than the bags you normally use for putting your sandwiches in. It is worth buying a supply of various sizes of polythene bags for freezing. They are reusable to some extent.

Freezer tape will have to be bought specially: ordinary sticky tape tends to peel off in a freezer (and is not much cheaper anyway). Labels, possibly colour-coded, will be needed.

freezer knife

These knives are specially designed to cut frozen food, a task which defeats ordinary kitchen knives. Wait and see whether you find yourself trying to cut up frozen food often enough to make it worthwhile buying such a knife. Be aware that a knife with a double-sided serration is more dangerous than a freezer saw.

rollers

Sets of rollers, that look something like skateboards, can be bought to put under the freezer so that it can be moved easily for cleaning. They are fitted with brakes for safety. Check that they will bear the weight of your freezer: the maximum recommended weight is usually about 600 lb.

cold box and ice packs

A cold box (also called cool box) is a useful accessory for a freezer owner, for getting frozen food home from the shops, when defrosting the freezer, as a standby in case of electricity failure, when moving home. It can also of course be used for picnics or for a camping holiday.

Cold (or cool) boxes are simply insulated boxes which slow down the rate at which their contents will warm up. (Those with polyurethane insulation, made of yellowy hardened foam, are better than those with polystyrene, white slabs, insulation; but only on a few is there information about what insulation is used.) Cold (or ice) packs are used to slow down this process even more.

Look for a cold box that closes firmly, preferably with a catch which pulls the lid on even tighter as it closes. Look, too, for one with good strong carrying handles. It will be heavy when fully loaded.

Cold packs or ice packs are also a useful buy, although you can get by with freezing water in other containers. Ice packs are sealed plastic sachets filled with a liquid designed to store cold (or, if you should want to, heat). You simply put them in a freezer or the frozen food compartment of a refrigerator for about 6 hours before you want to use them.

Buying secondhand

In the small ads of virtually every newspaper, there are freezers for sale. Before contacting anyone who is selling a secondhand freezer, do your homework. Sort out the priorities: what features and size you must have, what you would like, and what you can ignore. Obviously, buying secondhand reduces the available choice, but do not make the mistake of buying one just because it is cheap, and then finding it does not suit you after all.

When buying secondhand, beware of 'bargain' chest freezers which were used commercially for the storage of icecream. These are usually only conservators for storing frozen food, not to be used for freezing-down fresh food.

Get to know the brand names, read the previous *Which?* reports on freezers. Get some advertising literature from the manufacturers. Go and look at some freezers in the shops: it is a good idea to know just how small a 6 cu ft freezer and how big a 14 cu ft one actually is before you set off to buy one.

Before phoning a likely seller, make a list of questions to ask. Such a list might include:

- why are you selling?
  An obvious reason is that the freezer is too big or too small. The family may have increased or decreased, or they may have bought one the wrong size for their needs. Another common reason for selling is that the people who are selling are moving house, or have redesigned their kitchen, so that their freezer is no longer suitable.
- what is the manufacturer and model number?
  With any luck you will have some information on this model, which will make some of the other questions superfluous.
- what are its external/internal dimensions?
  This can help you decide if it is the right size for your family, both in terms of what it holds and fitting into the place where you want to keep it.
- has it got – baskets, interior light, etc?
  or whatever features you want.
- how old is it?
  Age is the important factor above all others: compressors do not last for ever and replacement is expensive. The general life expect-

ancy of a compressor is about seven years although it may last for much longer, if you are lucky.

If the answers seem satisfactory, make an appointment to go and see it. Look at the general condition of the freezer – even if the appearance does not matter to you (perhaps because the freezer is to go in an outhouse), see if there is any rust, or any broken bits inside.

– *doorseal*

Take with you a strip of paper cut from an exercise book, approximately 1 inch wide and 8 or 9 inches long. This is not to convince the seller that you are mad, but merely to check the seal of the freezer door. To do this, open the door and place the strip of paper across the edge. Close the door and try to pull the paper out. You should feel some resistance as it comes out. If in doubt, before pulling the paper completely out hold the end and push it back in. If the seal is ok the paper will just crumple. But if you can push it back, the freezer has a poor doorseal. Try this test in several places, particularly at corners. (It may be worth practising this on your refrigerator before you set out.)

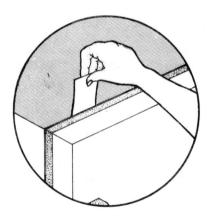

If the freezer is running and has been running for some time and you see a build-up of a lot of frost in some areas, this is a sign that the seal is poor.

A poor doorseal is not a grave disadvantage because on many models it can be replaced. You may be able to do this yourself.

– compressor

The most important thing when buying a secondhand freezer is to listen to it. The noise a freezer makes is more obvious when the compressor is switching on and off. If it does so very often, you are likely to notice the noise. A noisy compressor can be very irritating, and, more importantly, an increase in noise is often a significant advance warning of trouble in a compressor. It is impossible to judge how long a noisy compressor will last, so, it is probably not worth taking a gamble unless the asking price is very low.

Some of the noise (particularly when it switches on and off) may be due to vibration: the tubes at the back may have been bent, so that they knock against each other. Try holding the tubes, and check whether the noise is reduced. The cause may be that the rubber pads which cushion the vibration of the compressor have perished. (The rubber pads can be replaced by the service engineer.)

Ask the people who are selling the freezer whom they have called in to service their freezer – not whether they have used a service engineer – and whether they would recommend him. The answer may be illuminating.

Try and delay the decision whether to buy until you have heard the compressor switch itself off. (If the seller has stopped using the freezer and switches it on just for you, this may be difficult, particularly if it is a large freezer which takes a long time to cool down). It is useful, however, to make a rough note of how many minutes the compressor runs and for how many minutes it is off. Compressors vary, but in a room temperature of about 20°C (68°F), the 'on' time should be slightly less than the 'off' time. If the 'on' time is much greater than the 'off' time, do not buy – it may be a sign of future trouble.

– old model

When buying secondhand, you may come across some models which have storage space in the door. If you decide to buy one of these, you will have to be careful what you store there, because every time you open the door, whatever you keep there is exposed to room temperature and begins to warm up fairly quickly. This means that food cannot be stored there for as long as in the main body of the freezer.

– moving the freezer

If you decide to buy secondhand, think how you will get it home.

getting a freezer home

Freezers, even when empty, are quite heavy, and the sides are hard and slippery. If you decide to collect your own from the shop or warehouse, or buy one secondhand, some sort of porter's trolley will save much time and energy.

Dropping a freezer or rough handling can cause serious faults in the compressor. A faulty compressor usually has to be replaced by a service engineer and will cost between a third and half the price of a new freezer. Damage to any of the pipework could lead to loss of the refrigerant so that the machine would then not work without first being repaired.

Bumps and knocks can crack the insulation that keeps warm air out; the compressor would have to work harder to remove the extra warmth and this may reduce the life of the freezer. Or if the extra warmth is not detected by the thermostat of the freezer, there may be a warm area within the freezer and any food stored there will not last as long.

Freezers should be kept upright. If it is tilted more than about 30° in any direction the drier unit may become blocked. Replacing the drier unit would probably cost more than hiring a suitable vehicle in which to transport the freezer.

Wrap a blanket around the freezer to guard against the surface getting scratched. Apart from being unsightly, scratch marks are likely to start rusting.

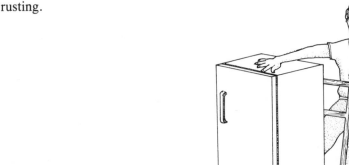

When the new freezer arrives

The freezer has been bought and has just been delivered. What next? There is usually some packaging around the freezer cabinet which has to be removed; at the back, packing is often put around the compressor to prevent it moving and that too must be taken out; or there may be transit screws that have to be slackened.

The lid or door is usually taped closed and sometimes a thin piece of wood has been put in to prevent it closing completely. The door seal sometimes gets squashed at this point. If so, pull it carefully so that it will seal properly. Inside, baskets and drawers are likely to be taped into position and have to be freed.

Also inside, there may be a booklet on home freezing and there should be an instruction book. Read this carefully, and note in particular the recommendations for the gaps to leave, and the setting for the thermostat. Make a note of the information on the rating plate and the date you bought the freezer, to save time later when service is required. Also, make a note of where and how the packing pieces were placed, in case you have to transport the freezer at a later date, for example when moving house. Keep the instruction book in a safe place.

Hopefully, there are no problems in positioning the freezer as this has already been decided, and no mistakes have been made with the tape measure.

It is a good idea, when you add the telephone number of the service department to your household list of useful addresses, to write down next to it the manufacturer, model and serial number of your new freezer.

SMITH RIFRIGERATION LTD				
gross volume	294 litres	10·4 cu ft	**model**	AZ316
storage volume	271 LITRES	9·6 cu ft	**serial no.**	652-741
freezing rate	18·2 kg/ 24 hrs		V 200/240 W	220
	40·0 1b/ 24 hrs			
Industrial Estate, Cringe, Yorks NQT 555.				

before plugging in

Obviously, an electric socket needs to be fairly near the freezer. It is better to avoid plugging a freezer into one side of a double socket, because someone may switch off both after using the other socket. To avoid any switching off by mistake, the plug and switch can be taped over. Alternatively, the freezer can be wired-in directly.

Consider wiring the freezer on a separate circuit. This has the advantage that when you go away, the electricity in the rest of the house can be disconnected by removing all the other fuses. If you run a separate ring main, you can plug into it freezer and refrigerator and other things you may want to leave on while you are away, such as an automatic greenhouse watering system, time-switch control, anti-burglar lights, telephone-answering machine (if this needs mains electricity). Then the fuses on the other ring mains can be pulled out.

Put a plug on the freezer lead if one has not been supplied. If the freezer has an unusual 2-pin plug, known as a continental type, do not attempt to plug it in. While you may get it in the socket, the earth line will not be connected and if a fault develops it could be dangerous – the whole cabinet could be at 240V and the electrical shock could kill. Cut off the plug and wire on a normal plug. But if there is no earth connection in the lead, consult the supplier or an electrician.

Freezers need a 13 amp fuse. The current taken by the pump when it starts is up to five times greater than when it just goes on running. This means that a fuse of a higher rating is needed than would appear necessary from the running wattage of a freezer: a 13 amp fuse rather than a 3 amp fuse.

Put the freezer in its place and make sure that there is the right space behind. Check that the freezer does not slide backwards when you lean on it. Visitors often lean against things in other people's kitchens, and the freezer is a comfortable leaning post. A freezer when full is heavy and, while it may easily slide back against the wall, it is difficult to pull foward again, So, do something about it now; a couple of pieces of wood might be the answer.

– get it level

A freezer should be level, to work efficiently and quietly. Some models have feet which can be adjusted: with the others, you may have to use small pieces of packing or wood underneath. Remember though, there is going to be a lot of weight on each piece, so avoid thin plywood or anything which is likely to collapse.

To check that the freezer is level in both directions, if you do not have a spirit level, you can use a saucer which you place in the bottom of the chest freezer, or on a shelf in an upright or fridge-freezer. Fill it with water and drip a drop of cooking oil into the middle. If the blob of oil moves, this shows that the freezer is not level.

– get it ready

Once the freezer is in position, wipe the inside to remove that stale smell. Use a warm solution of bicarbonate of soda (1 level tablespoon to 2 pints of water) – or just plain water. Do not use detergents because they can damage the inside: the chemical and the lining can react with each other. Dry completely, with a dry cloth and then leave the door or lid open to the air.

Do not switch on the freezer straightaway: the oil in the compressor must settle first. The longer you allow, the better – two hours is the very least

Now the freezer can be switched on. Tape the plug and switch, if possible, so that no-one will switch it off or unplug it by mistake. If there is a temperature warning light, which goes out when the temperature is too high, or a mains-on light, check that they come on when the freezer is switched on. If the light is not noticeable enough to catch your eye as you move around the kitchen, you will have to make a habit of checking that everything is ok. If the freezer is in the garage or outhouse, make a point of checking whenever you go to the freezer.

Set the thermostat at the setting recommended in the instructions. Leave the freezer running for at least 12 hours before introducing any food to make sure that everything is satisfactory. Be patient.

– getting the right temperature inside a freezer

If the freezer is not equipped with a thermometer, you should buy one. It does not cost a lot and will probably save you money in the long run. If the thermometer is not built-in, place it as close as possible to the top of the freezer, near the front. After the freezer has been running for 12 hours or so, check the temperature. It should be −18°C or 0°F. If it is more than a degree or so warmer than this (ie −17°C or 1°F), the freezer is too warm and the thermostat needs to be turned to a colder setting.

During the next few weeks, check the temperature inside frequently. Move the thermometer to different parts of the freezer to find the place where the freezer is least cold. In a chest freezer, this is likely to be just underneath the lid. With upright freezers, the warmest spot is not so easy to find. In general, it occurs at the top (because warm air rises), but manufacturers often concentrate the evaporator near the top. This removes the warm spot, but there may be others, in the middle or even at the bottom. If you do not find much difference in the various parts of the freezer, that is all to the good.

Ideally, the thermostat of the freezer should be set to give a temperature of −18°C (0°F) at the least cold spot, so that the whole freezer is colder than this. The setting needed for the thermostat depends on many things – in particular the temperature around the freezer and whether there is sufficient circulation of air to remove the waste heat. This means that the setting given by the manufacturer can only be a rough guide. You should adjust your thermostat until you find the ideal setting; but leave about three to four hours if the freezer is empty, about 12 hours if it is full before adjusting or readjusting.

When you are doing a lot of cooking and the kitchen is very warm, you must remember to check that the freezer remains at the right temperature.

– getting the right temperature in a fridge-freezer

In a fridge-freezer with a single compressor, there is only one thermostat to control both the refrigerator and the freezer temperatures. The temperature sensor for the thermostat which turns the compressor on and off is in the main part of the refrigerator. This can cause a problem. If the thermostat is set too cold, milk and other liquids may start to freeze in the refrigerator; too warm, and the contents of the freezer will not keep as long as they should.

Make a point of checking the temperature in the freezer part when the kitchen is cold, for example in the early morning after a cold night. If the kitchen gets too cold (less than 16°C, 61°F, as many kitchens do), the temperature in the freezer part will rise, because the thermostat will have switched off the compressor. When the temperature in the main part of the refrigerator rises above, say, 6°C (42°F), the thermostat will turn on the compressor and this will cool down the refrigerator and the freezer. But if the temperature outside the refrigerator drops to below 6°C, the temperature in the refrigerator part will not rise above 6°C and the compressor will not be turned on, so that no cooling will take place. This causes no problem in the refrigerator section, but the temperature in the freezer part will gradually rise and any food that is in it will be affected.

Normally, kitchen temperature is unlikely to fall below 6°C (42°F), but it might if you were to go away for some time during the depths of winter and switched off all the heating in the house.

The manufacturers' instructions draw attention to the importance of not installing single-compressor fridge-freezers in a cold place, but do not warn that at very low temperatures the mechanism will not work at all.

Organisation of the freezer

It is only too easy to get into a complete muddle with a freezer. A common problem is knowing that there is an apple pie in there somewhere, but where? Food which has overstayed its time lies hidden at the bottom. Once frozen, some foods can look exactly the same; while lamb stew may be defrosted instead of beef stew without great consequences, it becomes wasteful when chicken stock is defrosted instead of apple purée, or salmon mousse instead of rhubarb fool.

Whenever you open the door or lid of a freezer, the temperature insides warms up a bit, slightly less so in a chest freezer. This economy is lost if the chest freezer is badly organised, so that you have to keep the lid open for 5 minutes while searching for something. Things are usually easier to find in an upright and the door is therefore open for a shorter time.

It is a common misconception to blame extra running costs of an upright freezer on cold air falling out each time you open the door; you could open the door 100 times for under 2p of electricity. The reason why many upright freezers cost more to run is that their insulation is not as good as that of most chest freezers.

When you put goods into the freezer and take some out, remember to take out first so as not to submerge the article you intended to remove.

It is useful to have a flat surface on the door-opening side of an upright freezer on which to deposit removable shelves or chest baskets, so that the door or lid can be shut while you select what you want to take out.

packing and labelling

To organize the freezer, every package should be marked with
– contents (eg coq au vin)
  perhaps adding the quantity, either in number of portions or in weight
–date of freezing
  perhaps adding a 'use by' date.

If, as well as contents and date of freezing, a 'use by' date is written on the label (and in a notebook), it saves mental calculations every time the item is considered. If you write a 'use by' date also on bought frozen food, it will save you wondering which packet you bought when, particularly if you discover several identical packets lurking at the bottom of the freezer.

A chinagraph pencil or a waterproof 'freezer' pen, will not wipe off the label. You can buy special labels for use in a freezer. Alternatively, when buying freezer tape (which you will need to seal packages) buy the white type so that you can write on that. Some polythene bags designed for the freezer have white patches for writing on directly.

A suitable method if you freeze only a few types of food in roughly equal amounts, is to mark the bag, container or label with waterproof pen and make a chart on a piece of paper with the same information. Cross them off when used and when you next freeze food of the same kind, or put in frozen food, remember to record it.

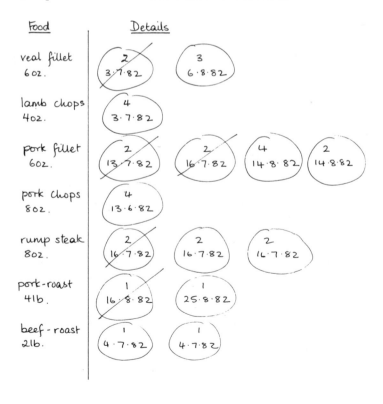

Food	Details			
veal fillet 6 oz.	2 3·7·82	3 6·8·82		
lamb chops 4oz.	4 3·7·82			
pork fillet 6oz.	2 13·7·82	2 16·7·82	4 14·8·82	2 14·8·82
pork chops 8oz.	4 13·6·82			
rump steak 8oz.	2 16·7·82	2 16·7·82	2 16·7·82	
pork-roast 4lb.	1 16·8·82	1 25·8·82		
beef-roast 2lb.	1 4·7·82	1 4·7·82		

Or, for each item you freeze, write out two labels: the first to go on the package, and the second on the chart. The chart can be divided into several sections or you can make several charts, each representing one kind of food. The more extensive and varied the contents of your freezer, the more sections there should be, so that you can get a clear representation of what is in the freezer at any one time.

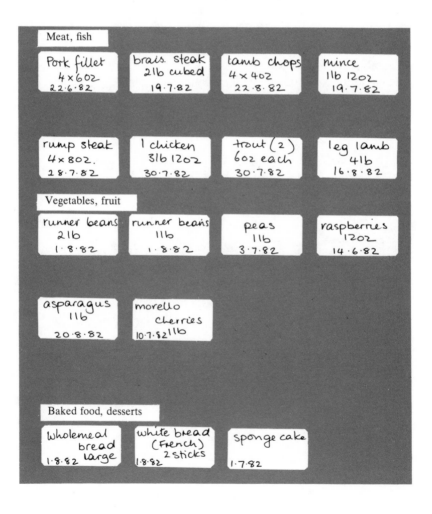

Meat, fish

Pork fillet	brais. steak	lamb chops	mince
4 x 6oz	2lb cubed	4 x 4oz	1lb 12oz
22.6.82	19.7.82	22.8.82	19.7.82

rump steak	1 chicken	trout (2)	leg lamb
4 x 8oz.	3lb 12oz	6oz each	4lb
28.7.82	30.7.82	30.7.82	16.8.82

Vegetables, fruit

runner beans	runner beans	peas	raspberries
2lb	1lb	1lb	12oz
1.8.82	1.8.82	3.7.82	14.6.82

asparagus	morello
1lb	cherries
20.8.82	10.7.82 1lb

Baked food, desserts

wholemeal	white bread	sponge cake
bread	(French)	
1.8.82 large	1.8.82 2 sticks	1.7.82

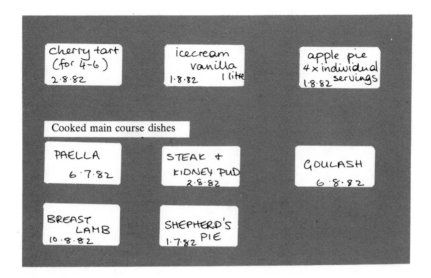

The various shelves or baskets in an upright freezer may be used for storing a particular kind of food. For example:
top shelf: bread, cakes, etc
2nd shelf: ready made meals, such as stew, risotto, etc.
3rd shelf: icecream and various sweets
4th shelf: meat
bottom: vegetables

A simple record can be kept in a small notebook, perhaps classified by the type of food keeping separate pages for meat, for vegetables, for baked items and so on. Cross off items as you use them. It is a good idea to tie a pencil to the notebook and to keep it near the freezer or even attached to it.

As things are used up they can be crossed out. This ensures that packages are not forgotten and that food is used in rotation.

When you plan the meals for the coming week, take out your record of what is in the freezer and plan what to use up. Or if you do not

Date	Goods	Number & type of package	Details	Use by
29.6.82	Mint (3½oz dry mint & castor sugar) pestle and mortar treatment	foil (2) container	container divided by foil strips - contents of container 10oz (water absorbed after mint wash - better to pat dry with cloth)	29.6.92
18.7.82	Raspberries freeflow approx 2½lb	2 litre 1 container	John Parry 8oz used 25/8/82 8oz used 24/8/82 8oz used 19/9/82	18.5.83
25.7.82	Cauliflower (not blanched - washed & dried only)	4 bags X ✓✓	8oz bag used 11/9/82 ; 7½oz bag used ; 9oz bag used ; 11oz bag used	25.7.83
25.7.82	Peas - homegrown Hurst greenshaft	opaque white bags B	6oz used 11/10/82 ; 6oz used ; 6oz used 6oz used	25.7.83
FREEZER FULL!!				
3.8.82	Pulverised Costa Rica coffee	coffee bag	commenced 13/8/82 finished 28/9/82	
4.8.82	Whipping cream bought frozen	own pack	commenced 12/8/82 last 3½oz transferred to finished fridge freezer 17/9/82 fridge freezer	6.2.83
2.9.82	Homegrown tomato Eath 7oz	2x(2) poly bag	skinned de-seeded - not prepared in any way 1st used 28/10/82 2nd given away M.J. lost everything but colour	2.9.83
24.9.82	Bramble mousse base	foil (4) round	stewed blackberries, lemon, sugar only add gelatine (plus cream & egg whites)	24.9.83
24.9.82	Grated cheese	2 —?lbs	1st out ; 2nd out	"

make a menu-plan for the week ahead, look at your freezer record every day and consider which of the contents you might use today. Always remember that a steady turnover of the contents of the freezer helps to make good use of it and eliminates the danger of leaving things in too long.

– in a chest freezer

With a chest freezer, whatever the make and model, you can buy extra baskets and use a basket for each type of food. The usual method of organising the freezer is to have a row of baskets on the bottom, a row above them and a row at the top. If the top row has one basket missing, this means that by lifting only one basket every basket is accessible.

If there is a load line indicated in the freezer, do not store any food above it.

Finding a package can be made simpler by using different colour labels for different kinds of food, eg red for meat, blue for fish, green for vegetables. Alternatively, buy plastic bags in different colours. All meat can then be stored in the red bag, vegetables in the green bag, and so on. Whichever method you use, try and keep the freezer tidy so that food can be found quickly and easily. Do not behave like squirrels which bury their provisions for the winter and cannot find them again. Make it a rule, therefore, from the very beginning, to label everything that goes into the freezer.

There is another reason why you should keep your freezer tidy, particularly a chest freezer. The freezer is essentially a box, so usually only the sides are refrigerated. (Some uprights have refrigerated shelves which reduces this problem.) To keep things cold inside, the cold air must circulate, otherwise you risk some parts of the freezer not being cold enough. The portion just underneath the lid is particularly vulnerable. Every time the lid is opened, warm air gets in and forms a pocket at the top and if there is no air circulation inside, the warm air will warm up the food it is in contact with.

It takes a very long time for cold to penetrate food. If you were to fill a medium sized chest freezer full with fresh meat, leaving no room for air circulation, it would take nearly a month for the bits in the middle even to start to freeze.

packaging

Packaging is an essential part of preparing food for storing in a freezer, to prevent the loss of moisture from the food and to protect it.

Warm air can hold more moisture than cold air, as is shown by condensation forming when warm air meets a cold surface and moisture is deposited. In a freezer, a similar thing happens. It is inevitable that there are temperature differences inside a freezer, even if only a few degrees. Moisture from food is given up to the surrounding air and the air loses this vapour at the coldest part, near the evaporator plate. (This is the cause of the frost which builds up there.)

When too much moisture is removed from food, the food dries out, giving rise to 'freezer burn' – those whitish, discoloured patches, caused by dehydration, sometimes found on poorly wrapped items. Freezer burn in itself is harmless, it just makes the food drier and tougher.

Some foods have very characteristic and strong natural smells. If not wrapped properly, the smell can effect the flavour of other stored foods. Dairy products in particular are likely to pick up flavours from such goods as smoked meats, fish, cabbage, leeks and, to a lesser extent peas and beans.

Oxygen from the air reacts with fat in foods to form chemicals which give meat and fish a bad, rancid taste and smell. Fried foods and fat meat and fish can suffer from this problem when stored for a long time in the freezer. Good wrapping which excludes the air slows down this process, and therefore lengthens the storage time.

All food which is stored in the freezer must therefore be securely wrapped. The material used must be of a consistency and thickness to make the package as airtight as possible, and not split, tear or break easily.

The various types of packaging include:

– *thin plastic film* which clings to itself and to plastic and to metal and other materials can be used as lining, particularly if you want to freeze acidic or citric foods in foil; or as interleaving between slices of cooked meat or pancakes, so that one can be removed at a time; or to wrap individual portions of cakes or sandwiches, which have to be overwrapped in strong polythene for freezing. The special freezer film can also be used in microwave ovens, but should be pierced in a few places before cooking.

– *aluminium foil* is also convenient for wrapping awkward shaped items and excluding air, but tears more easily. Use the thicker, heavy-duty type to avoid this. Aluminium foil is not advised for wrapping acidic food such as fruits.

– *polythene* either bags or sheeting can be used. The stronger, heavy-duty varieties are usually advisable. (They are reusable.) They can be used to line a rigid container, such as a plastic box, and then moved out of the box when the contents have been frozen. This has the advantage of getting the food into a uniform shape for easy storage like a row of bricks and the box can be re-used.

Some varieties of polythene (sold in the name of boil-in-bags or similar) and nylon (roaster) bags which withstand the temperature of boiling water can also be used. They are particularly useful for such things as sauces, which can then be reheated by immersing the bag in boiling water. Saves washing up, too. But be careful: if you put ordinary polythene in boiling water, it will make a messy coating which could be impossible to remove from the food.

– *plastic boxes* are available in a variety of shapes and sizes. They can be specially bought, but many foods such as icecream are often sold in suitable containers, which can be reused. A supply of old 2 litre and 4 litre containers is easily acquired if the family eats lots of icecream. Being rectangular, they stack easily so that freezer space is used to advantage.

– *glass jars* are not really suitable for the freezer. Some jars are not strong enough to withstand the low temperatures in a freezer, and shatter.

– *foil dishes* are very useful as they are light, space saving and reusable. Pies made and frozen in foil dishes can be reheated in their containers. (But foil dishes without a lid, or with an ill-fitting one, must be overwrapped or put in a bag.) Foil dishes cannot be used for reheating in a microwave oven, because the foil deflects the microwaves. A special freezer-to-microwave dish made of coated paper should be used instead, or the pie transferred to a suitable container.

butcher's wrap

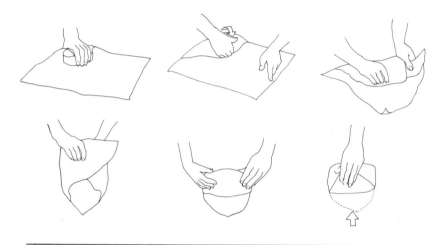

druggist's wrap

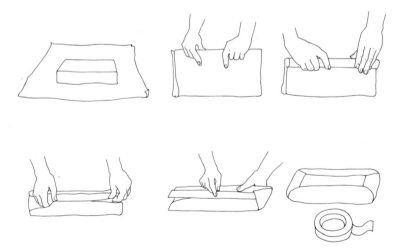

how to wrap

There are basically two methods of wrapping:

butcher's wrap: place the food close to one corner of a large sheet. Fold this corner over the food, give the package a complete turn, bring the slides over the centre, and continue to roll the package to the opposite corner. Seal with freezer tape.

druggist's wrap: place the food in the centre of a sheet. Allow enough to cover it, plus 3 to 4 inches, about 10 cm, to overlap. Bring the longer edges together over the food, and fold the edges over and over so that the wrapping is folded tightly against the food. Fold in the shorter ends and seal with freezer tape.

Overwrapping gives extra protection. For example, wrap a joint first in foil and then in a plastic bag. This ensures that air is excluded, even if the outer layer becomes damaged.

If the final layer of wrapping is transparent, a label can be slipped inside, before sealing. This allows larger writing or more details than on the commercially available freezer labels.

Leave a gap at the top of containers when freezing liquids. Liquids expand on freezing and if insufficient space is left, the lid will be pushed off or the container broken. The surface can be protected from air by a layer of foil or film, which will move as the liquid expands.

A crumpled layer of foil or film will keep solids below the surface of the liquid (in fruit salad, for instance), and prevent discolouration.

getting the air out

Fill the bag and press gently to exclude as much air as possible.

Another way of removing air is to dip the unsealed bag in water – the water pressure forces the air out. But remember to dry the bag before putting it in the freezer otherwise it will need chipping out.

Air can be sucked out of the bag, perhaps through a straw inserted into the bag before twisting the neck of the bag and sealing it.

sealing

Sealing is essential to keep the package from unwrapping and allowing air to get inside. There are several methods:

with freezer tape: this sticky tape, usually colourless or white, has a special adhesive so that, unlike ordinary tape which sticks only on dry surfaces, it remains stuck at the low temperatures inside a freezer.

with wire tags: polythene bags which have been sealed with freezer tape often tear when the tape is removed, and are thus not reusable. Plastic or paper-coated wire for fastening the package is therefore better in this respect. These twist-ties which go round the neck of bags can also be reused. Do not use wire tags in a microwave oven.

You have to be careful not to pierce the bag when using plastic or paper-covered wire tags for sealing polythene bags: fold the ends inwards so that the wires are covered.

Twist the neck of the bag, fold over the top and twist the wire round firmly. Twist the ends of the wires together.

by heat sealing: there are some special heat sealers on the market but bags are not reusable if sealed in this way.

Avoid rubber bands: they are likely to perish.

useful hints

When the instructions say 'pack in a rigid container', you can use margarine tubs and the flower-pot shaped containers with a lid in which you have bought yogurt or cottage cheese, which come in various sizes. The larger ones could be used for soups or casseroles, the smaller ones for freezing leftovers. Round containers take up more room; the flower-pot ones can be stored upside down.

making bricks without straw

Rectangular shapes make the most economical use of space because they can be stacked without gaps. To make polythene bags into rectangular shapes, line a rigid container (such as a sugar carton, fruit juice carton, cereal box) with a polythene bag of the appropriate size. Fill with the food (if it is liquid leave a headspace), and seal. When it is frozen, remove the brick or cube in its polythene bag from the container and store.

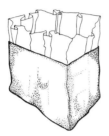 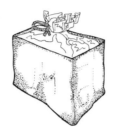 

If small quantities are involved, for instance using one-portion cereal packets for freezing individual portions, the little frozen bags can be stored together in a larger plastic box, such as a 2-litre icecream container.

Prepare a casserole in ovenproof ware, and when cool transfer to the freezer. If you do not want to have a dish out of action in the freezer, line the dish with foil, before you put in the ingredients for cooking the casserole. Then after cooling and freezing, the contents in the foil can be removed from the dish and overwrapped in strong foil or polythene. Alternatively, cook in the ordinary way, remove the casserole from the freezer after about 12 hours and place the dish in warm water; the frozen contents can be removed from the dish. Wrap well in foil or plastic film, overwrap and replace in the freezer. To thaw, the frozen block can be placed back in the dish. Bear in mind that if a quantity suitable for say 6 people is frozen in one block, it has to be thawed in one go. Therefore, cook, cool, and divide into portions for four and two, or three and three, and freeze in suitable boxes or bags. Write the number of portions on the label and if you have visitors you can thaw the lot, or just one or two as needed.

When cooking shepherds pie in bulk, prepare the pie in a large roasting tin and freeze until just firm. Then cut into bricks of a convenient size. Double wrap each 'brick' tightly, and return to the freezer.

interleaving

Interleave things such as chops or sandwiches with pieces of foil or film, so that they will then separate easily without thawing.

Waxed paper, if you can find a supply, is useful – not so much for packing but for lining baking sheets for open-freezing, for separating baked goods during storage, and so on. It is worth saving the linings from cereal packets where these are still of waxed paper.

Ice cube trays are useful for freezing very small quantities (such as baby food). Once frozen, the cubes can be removed and stored in polythene bags.

open-freezing

Many foods can be open-frozen on a tray, without packing – for instance sausages, some vegetables and fruit. As soon as they are frozen, they have to be packed in a polythene bag or container. The advantage of open-freezing (also called free-flow) is that single portions or as much as or as little as you may want can be removed and used.

making the most

A freezer can store ingredients that are fiddly to prepare:

– *breadcrumbs*
Fresh breadcrumbs go mouldy quickly, but keep well in the freezer and thaw quickly. Supermarkets often sell day-old white bread quite cheaply and it is worth buying some and setting up the blender to prepare a large quantity of breadcrumbs. Pack in 2 oz or 4 oz (50 g or 100 g) quantities and draw on them for treacle tarts, stuffings, meat loaf and so on.

– *grated cheese*
Similarly, supermarkets sometimes sell off 'time-expired' cheese at a reduced price. A couple of pounds can be grated and packed in a polythene bag, or in various small bags, and will then be ready for cooking or making sauces or gratin dishes.

– duchesse potatoes
It is worthy dirtying a forcing-bag and pipe for a large quantity (say ½ stone, 3 kg). Pipe out onto a tray covered with waxed paper, open-freeze and store in rigid containers. They are useful and impressive for visitors; glaze before thawing, if you want to show off.

– anything chocolate
Dealing with chocolate makes for messy washing up, so when next you are making, say, butter cream icing, mix up extra quantities for freezing.

– crumble topping
When you use the mixer (or your hands) to make some, make up a lot. It freezes well and thaws quickly.

– cream
Cream does not freeze well, but double or whipping cream lightly sweetened and whipped just to a peak can be piped into rosettes, open-frozen on waxed paper covered baking sheets and subsequently stored in plastic boxes. The rosettes can be placed, still frozen, on trifles or jellies or flans and allowed to thaw in situ.

– stock
When you have bulk-bought meat, grit your teeth and deal with the bones: make stock, reduce well and pack into a rigid container with a plastic bag inside. When frozen, the stock 'brick' can be removed from the box, labelled, overwrapped and will store neatly in the freezer; worth it, in the long run, compared with stock cubes.

– wine
When decanting red wine, have a container handy and as soon as the sediment moves towards the neck of the bottle, pour the cloudy wine into the container. It can be frozen – not for drinking, but for use in a casserole or stew.

– coffee
Coffee beans can be frozen provided they are freshly roasted; overwrapped because of the smell. For making iced coffee, cool strong

black coffee can be frozen in ice-cube trays; then store in polythene bags and add one or two of the frozen cubes when making iced coffee.

– herbs
Herbs, freshly picked, can be frozen. Wash and either freeze whole or remove leaves from stalks and chop finely and pack into small containers. Blanching the leaves for ½ min darkens the colour, unblanched herbs look brown after frozen storage.

– mint
Strip tender mint leaves from their stems, remove the large veins. Wash, pat dry, chop coarsely, use (if available) a pestle and mortar to crush leaves with one teaspoonful of castor sugar and a sprinkle of salt to 2 ounces of leaves, reduce to a pulp. Freeze in small plastic containers, or icecube tray. To use, put into a screwtop jar, add vinegar (wine for preference) and shake occasionally while it thaws.

metric/imperial conversion

1 lb (16 oz) = 454 g	1 kg (1000 g) = 2 lb 3¼ oz
1 oz = 28.35 g	100 g = 3½ oz
1 ft = 30.48 cm	1 m (1000 mm) = 3 ft 3⅜ in
1 in = 2.54 cm	1 cm (10 mm) = ⅜ in
0°F = −17.8°C	0°C = 32°F

To convert °C to °F subtract 32, multiply by 5 and divide by 9.
To convert °F to °C multiply by 9, divide by 5 and add 32.

ft = foot	lb = pound	kg = kilogram	m = metre
in = inch	oz = ounce	g = gram	cm = centimetre
			mm = millimetre

How cold is a freezer?

A basic requirement of any freezer is that it should keep frozen food at below 0°F (below −18°C). It should also be able to freeze fresh food to 0°F, −18°C, or below, within 24 hours. If freezing takes longer, there is likely to be some loss of flavour or texture. The faster the freezing is to −18°C (0°F), the better.

Domestic refrigerators and freezers are rated with stars according to the temperature at which (and therefore the length of time for which) they are able to keep the food.

A * compartment is at −6°C and will keep already frozen food for up to a week.
A ** compartment is at −12°C and will keep already frozen food for up to a month.
A *** compartment is at −18°C and will keep already frozen food for at least 3 months. If sold as a separate appliance, a three-star cabinet is known as a conservator. It should not be used for freezing fresh food because it does not do so fast enough.

A * *** compartment or appliance is usually kept at −18°C and will keep already frozen food for at least 3 months. The extra star, however, means that it is also capable of going down to temperatures of approximately −25°C to −30°C, the right temperatures at which to freeze down fresh food.

Although ice cubes can be made in any frozen food compartment, you should not attempt to freeze fresh food in any but a * *** appliance.

Freezing

Most fresh foods contain over 60% water, some of which is tightly bound up within the cells that make up the food. Most of the water moves freely within the food and it is this water which freezes. Pure water freezes at 0°C (32°F) but the water in food freezes at temperatures a little lower than this because of the sugars and salts dissolved in it.

The freezing zone at which ice crystals begin to form is between 0°C and −6°C. The longer food is held in this temperature range during freezing, the more the quality of the food is affected.

If food is frozen slowly, large ice crystals form. Large crystals break open the cells, so that when the food thaws, this water can escape, and the quality of the food is lost. It is the cellular structure that collapses, producing, for instance, 'mushy' strawberries on thawing. If the food is frozen quickly, the crystals which form within the cells are small and can melt again without breaking the cells within the food. It is therefore important that the time taken for the food to freeze is kept as short as possible.

how to freeze

- Allow any cooked food to cool to at least room temperature, then put it into the refrigerator if you have one before freezing.
- Package the food correctly beforehand, unless open-freezing.
- Freeze in small quantities; it may be better, when freezing a large quantity, to put only half in the freezer and keep the other half in the refrigerator until the first lot is frozen-down.
- Place foods to be frozen as close as possible to the evaporator plate (or on to the freezing-down shelf or into the freezing-down compartment) so that the warmth is removed as quickly as possible. Anything that is stored there should be put into another part of the freezer.
- Use the fast-freeze (super) switch when freezing-down more than a couple of pounds. The fast-freeze switch overrides the thermostat, so that the temperatures inside the freezer can go on falling to about −27°C. The colder the freezer, the quicker the food will freeze. It takes about 6 hours for the freezer to fall from its normal −18°C to −27°C (it may take longer if the freezer is already full).

If you are planning to do a lot of freezing, switch on the fast-freeze at least 6 hours beforehand (and leave it on until 24 hours after the load is put in). When unfrozen food is added into the freezer, the food around it is made less cold. Switching on the fast-freeze in advance and making the food that is already stored in the freezer as cold as possible (−27°C) before adding a fresh supply, means that the 'old' is not warmed up to above −18°C and its own coldness helps towards the freezing of the 'new' supply.

It is the ability of * *** freezers to reach temperatures as cold as −27°C or less that is important in freezing food. The faster the food is frozen, the better its quality will be. The temperature in a freezer rises slightly when unfrozen food is put in and this means that anything other than a * *** freezer cannot cope with the sudden increase in internal temperature: the freezing-down process would take too long, and the quality of the food would be affected.

storage times

Freezing does not completely stop the normal processes of deterioration, it merely slows them down. But because it happens so slowly, it is difficult to determine exactly when the food passes its best. The maximum storage times quoted in books on freezing and on packages of ready-frozen foods have been determined by various people, using their personal judgment as to when they can detect the changes which signify the food is past its best. So remember that storage times quoted – even in this book – are only a rough guide and should not be taken as gospel.

Frozen food which has been stored for longer than the 'recommended' time is not necessarily bad – it is just past its prime. If in doubt, thaw the item and apply the usual visual, smelling and tasting tests that you would to fresh food. A cake may be a little soggy or vegetables less tasty, but they are probably perfectly ok for family use, even if not for special guests.

The longer the recommended storage time, the more relaxed you can be in sticking to it. If the recommended life is 12 months, then it is unlikely that you would detect any difference for another couple of months. But when the storage time is as little as 1 month, deterioration would be fairly obvious after a further couple of months. The colour and smell of the food may have changed, its flavour faded or gone slightly 'off', or its texture may have altered for the worse. On the whole, if food has deteriorated so much that it would cause a tummy upset, its appearance or smell would, as with non-frozen food, have put you off eating it.

lessening the changes which occur in frozen food

Vegetables can develop a hay-like 'off' flavour within a short time. Brussels sprouts, for example, even if frozen can begin to show the first signs of deterioration after only a few days. However, if the vegetables are first immersed in boiling water for a few minutes (a process known as blanching) the slight enzyme activity which continues in food despite the low temperature, is stopped.

With fruits, blanching is seldom used since it would destroy the delicate flavours and texture. Fruit which is cooked before freezing usually keeps better.

The fats in meat, fish and pastry products can still react with the air at low temperatures, and can get rancid. Wrapping food well and excluding the air can improve the storage life.

Spices and seasonings change with time. The true flavour of spices begins to fade after three or four months storage and becomes a nondescript peppery flavour. Curries will mellow and if used after more than about 2 months freezer storage, may need to be improved with freshly ground spices. On the other hand, salt appears to increase in intensity and it is therefore advisable to be mean with the salt when preparing dishes.

Herbs tend to lose their impact after a couple of months, so if your casserole depends on that touch of rosemary, either do not leave it too long in the freezer or add the herbs when – slowly – reheating.

Garlic can become very bitter after a couple of months and completely spoil the dish. Again, reheat slowly and add then.

what not to freeze

Not all foods are suitable for freezing.

salads

After freezing, all vegetables lose some of their crispness. This means that lettuce, cucumber, tomatoes, celery which were stored in a freezer cannot subsequently be used in a salad. However, they can all be used as an ordinary cooking vegetable; even lettuce can be used, like spinach.

mayonnaise, cream, egg custards, milk puddings

Foods of this type tend to separate when frozen. During freezing, the water contents form ice crystals which separate from the fatty solids and may not emulsify again even if the food is vigorously stirred, certainly not if unstirred. However, double cream keeps better than single, especially when a little sugar has been added. If you particularly want to freeze these foods (perhaps because they are leftovers which would otherwise be thrown away), when it comes to using, thaw slowly in a refrigerator, whisking well afterwards. It sometimes works – at other times, you can be left with a horrible mess. Much depends on the proportion of fat.

Cream can be bought ready-frozen; it is sometimes sold as a bag of pieces, which can be very useful as a standby.

eggs

Freezing whole eggs causes the shells to shatter. But spare egg yolks and whites will freeze, particularly if a little sugar or salt is added (but make sure you write on the label what you have added).

macaroons, soft meringues, royal icing and frostings without fat

These tend to thaw into a horrible soggy mess.

jam

This loses its 'set' on freezing. If you have a glut of fruit for jam-making, freeze the fruit, either raw or cooked. Keep it for up to 3 months after freezing, thaw and make the jam in the normal way.

refreezing

On the whole, refreezing is not recommended, because the process of thawing and refreezing spoils the flavour and texture of food. However, food from the freezer can be used to make up a dish, which, after cooking, is frozen.

Food storage: a guide to temperatures

micro-organisms causing food poisoning	micro-organisms causing spoilage eg moulds	enzymes affecting taste and texture	°C	
fast growth	fast growth	fast activity	25	
			20	range of normal kitchen temperatures
			15	
			10	cool larder
slow growth			5 — 7 — 4	normal temperature in main compartment of domestic refrigerator
			0	water freezes
	slow growth		−5 — −6	✳ store frozen food for up to 1 week
			−10	
			−12	✳✳ store frozen food for up to 1 month
			−15	
			−20 — −18	✳✳✳ store frozen food for up to 3 months
			−25	
dormant	dormant	slow activity	−27	✳ ✳✳✳
			−30	
			−35 — −34	food frozen commercially
			−40	
		inactive	−45	

Thawing

Food should not be eaten straight from the freezer.

cooking from frozen

Many foods can be safely cooked straight from the freezer. Indeed, many taste better that way.

Vegetables: add straight to boiling water, counting the cooking time from the moment the water returns to the boil.

Joints: these can be cooked straight from the freezer, with the exception of meat which has been boned and rolled.

A joint will take longer to cook from frozen and care must be taken to ensure that it is thoroughly cooked. A meat thermometer can help. All meat which is to be grilled can be put directly under the grill in its frozen state. Casseroles and dishes with a bolognese sauce can be re-heated successfully from frozen. Run tap water over the container to warm it sufficiently to allow the food to be got out. Put the food in a thick-bottomed saucepan with a little water, and cover with a lid. Place on a low heat. Stir occasionally to help break it up and ensure it does not catch and burn (add more water if necessary). Do not try to break up lumps that are frozen solid; give it time to soften.

thawing in the refrigerator

Food intended to be eaten while still frozen, such as icecream, is best not eaten immediately it is removed from the freezer because the very low temperature affects both the flavour and texture. If it is kept in a refrigerator for about half an hour before being eaten, both the flavour and texture are improved.

If in doubt about thawing any food, thaw overnight in the refrigerator. The exception to this is fruit: most fruits, particularly soft berries, taste better if they still have a cold 'edge' to them and thawing for a couple of hours at room temperature is about right.

It is important that poultry is fully thawed in the refrigerator before roasting. This is because there is a slight risk that the oven heat may not penetrate right into the middle where dormant micro-organisms may be hidden. Leave the chicken (or other food to be slow-thawed) in its wrapping, so that it will not drip. Even so, put the food that is thawing below cooked food in a refrigerator, not on the shelf above other food.

A large frozen turkey or chicken transferred to the refrigerator for gradual thawing can reduce the refrigerator temperature and freeze or cause damage to the contents of the refrigerator, such as glass bottles cracking.

thawing at room temperature

Inevitably this is quicker than thawing in the refrigerator, but should be avoided for foods which can go off quickly, such as pork and poultry.

speeding up thawing

Thawing can be speeded up, if the food (well wrapped and sealed) is placed in a bowl of lukewarm water. As the water cools, it can be replaced. Do not be tempted to use hot water: it would result in the thawing being uneven and too rapid to preserve the texture.

– in a microwave oven
Thawing in a microwave oven takes a fraction of any other thawing time.

Microwaves are high-frequency, short-length waves generated by a magnetron inside the oven. The waves are reflected by metal and bounce off the sides of the oven, passing straight through materials such as plastic and glass. They are absorbed by anything which contains any moisture including, therefore, food. It is the high frequency waves that produce the changes in microwave oven cooking.

Microwaves can penetrate food to about 1–2 in only. Ice absorbs microwaves very slowly. So, when thawing frozen food, if there is no 'defrost' or 'pulsing' setting, the microwave oven must be switched on and off manually at the requisite intervals to establish a regular sequence of rest (off) and energy (on). If the frozen food were continually bombarded by microwaves, without the 'rest' intervals, the outside would cook but the inside of the food remain frozen.

Maintenance

A freezer requires very little in the way of attention, but that does not mean that it can be ignored.

– between defrosts

If the loose frost that builds up inside a freezer is scraped off, you can delay a full defrost. Do this with the plastic scraper which is usually provided with your freezer. If one was not, or if you have lost it, buy another; they are not expensive. Do not use something like a metal knife: it can cut into the paint inside, and expose the metal which, unless it is aluminium, will then start to rust. Or it may cut through the plastic, allowing moisture to get into the insulation – wet insulation does not keep the cold in or the heat out. If you were really unlucky, you might even puncture one of the tubes carrying refrigerant and then it would be very unlikely that the freezer could be repaired.

Defrosting

The freezer ought to be defrosted when the build-up of ice gets to about, 5 mm ($\frac{1}{8}$ in to $\frac{1}{4}$ in) thick. That is usually after about 4–6 months for an upright, 12 months for a chest freezer. Try and choose a time when the freezer is low in stock. Although people often choose a hot day, thinking that it will be quicker to melt the ice, it is better to try and choose a relatively cold day.

- Turn the fast-freeze switch on about six hours before you start defrosting. The colder the food when you take it out of the freezer, the longer before it thaws.
- Put a pile of old newspapers in the freezer, and then use them to wrap up the frozen food when you take it out.
- Store the frozen food somewhere cool; using the refrigerator (turn thermostat setting to the coldest beforehand and remove the contents) is one idea. (Or if you have a coldbox, use that for the frozen food with the shortest life.) Putting the food outside on a cold winter's day is another; pack the food close together or into a cardboard box or laundry bin and cover with more newspapers or an old blanket.
- Switch off the freezer and, if you can, disconnect it from the mains; and leave the door or lid open. Or place bowls of hot water inside

and shut the door or lid to hasten the melting of the ice. Do not use an electric heater, this can be extremely dangerous not only because dripping water and electricity do not mix, but also because too much heat inside the freezer can damage it.

Put something down to collect the drip water. If your freezer has a drainage channel, a bowl can be used. On an upright freezer, you may need to place old newspapers or rags to stop the water flowing out onto the floor. If necessary, protect the floor with a sheet of polythene.

- As the ice begins to melt, the process can be helped along by using the plastic scraper.
- Never use salt or other chemicals to help the process; they are likely to damage the surfaces.
- Change the bowls of hot water when they start to cool off.
- When the ice has melted, wipe down all the surfaces with a cloth. Baie out any water that has accumulated in the bottom.

When defrosting a chest freezer without a drainage hole, spread an old towel in the base; when the thawing begins and sheets of frost can be eased off with the scraper, these can be lifted with the towel and disposed of. The towel will also absorb drip water so there will be less need for bailing out.

It may be desirable to remove any smells by wiping the inside with a mild solution of bicarbonate of soda (1 level tablespoon to 2 pints of water). Do not use soap or detergents.

- Finally, dry all the surfaces with a clean dry cloth.
- Switch on the freezer again and switch on the fast-freeze for about 10–15 minutes before reloading the freezer. But if you have had to leave the frozen food in a pile in the warm kitchen, reload the freezer immediately.
- Leave the fast-freeze on for another couple of hours even if the temperature warning light seems to show that the temperature is cold enough, to ensure that all the food is thoroughly cold again. If the fast-freeze is left on for a long time all it does is to use more electricity; it causes no harm except the slight extra expense.

The whole process of defrosting should generally take no longer than about an hour, but on a fixed-shelf upright freezer it can take up to two hours, because of the freezing element incorporated in the shelves.

reorganising

Defrosting time may be a good time to take stock of what is in the freezer. Renew labels and markings as necessary; packages that have lost their dating should be used up as quickly as possible. Find any missing packages and check that no storage times have been exceeded or are about to be exceeded. If so, put them in an easily accessible place and make a point of using them within the next few weeks. If you discover a forgotten package at the bottom of the freezer which has long outstayed its welcome, let your nose be your guide after thawing it. If in doubt, throw out.

If you keep a written record of the contents of the freezer, check that it is accurate and that you did not use up the last apple pie one day and forget to cross it off. If you do not keep a record, refresh your memory about what is in the freezer. Note what foods you are running short of, and what you have large stocks of so that you can use up some of it and not find yourself in June with a lot of frozen strawberries just when a bumper crop is appearing in the garden.

Make a note of the defrosting date in your freezer log book.

the outside of the cabinet

While the freezer is defrosting, it is a good idea to pay a little attention to the outside. Wipe it down with a damp cloth, using a small amount of detergent (not an abrasive powder or liquid), then wipe it with a dry cloth. If the condenser is a large black network at the back, it will collect dust, like everything else. Thick layers of dust prevent the heat escaping. Give the back a going-over with the vacuum cleaner but be careful not to do any damage to the pipes.

If you can move the freezer, clean the floor behind, and underneath it as well. Use a couple of rollers to help to move it forward. Remember that an upright freezer can tip over when being moved forward or back, and you may not be able to hold it – so, if possible get assistance, just in case.

If your freezer is in the kitchen, polishing is not really necessary, but it helps to preserve the surface and keep it shiny. If it is in a garage or outhouse, it is important to keep it well polished, to minimise the risk of rusting. Use a silicone polish – the sort designed for use on the car is suitable; apply sparingly and polish well.

rust

For a freezer kept in a garage or outhouse, rust can be enemy number one, and it also occurs in freezers kept in the kitchen. A little bit of rust would not be so important, but it usually spreads.

Rust can appear on the cabinet itself, or the working parts at the back or side. Treat rust on the cabinet in the same way as treating small areas of rust on the car:

- rub the area with a fine grade of emery paper to remove all traces of rust
- paint or spray the area with rust inhibitor, allow to dry thoroughly
- repaint with primer and then a couple of coats of enamel paint.

Treating rust on the black working parts can be more difficult, particularly if it has been allowed to get a hold. If you are sure it is just surface rust, it can be rubbed down and treated in the way described above. If there is the slightest doubt that the rust could have almost eaten through the metal, rubbing down could cause a hole to appear, and a hole – even if less than the size of a pinprick – can mean death to a freezer. The compressor itself is usually quite robust and the fins of the condenser are unimportant, but the tube which snakes down the back is made of quite thin metal and must not be punctured.

Other tubes at the back are usually made of copper and sometimes, particularly if some work has had to be done by a service engineer, there are signs of oxidation: a flaky white powder, perhaps coloured with bits of blue or green. This, too, can eat its way through the copper pipe. Rub down with a fine emergy paper to remove it.

If your freezer is kept in a garage or outhouse and the compressor is hidden behind a panel, it is worth inspecting it every couple of years so that any rust can be treated. Removing the panel may not be easy (it is usually held in by 4 screws which may be located in rather inaccessible places), but if it can be removed, it is worth the effort.

Do not forget to unplug the freezer before doing any work on it.

If things go wrong

On the whole, a freezer is a very reliable piece of household equipment. But the snag is that if it fails to work, you could lose a lot of money. If your dishwasher or washing machine fails, you may have to resort to washing by hand, if the vacuum cleaner fails, you might resign yourself to a dirtier than usual home until you get it fixed, but with a freezer, your food starts to deteriorate, and food costs money.

accidents

Within the working life of a freezer, it is highly probable that someone will fail to close the door properly, or absentmindedly switch off the freezer.

To help prevent accidents, put a piece of tape across the plug and switch. If you have to plug the freezer into one half of a double switched socket, try not to use the other half socket for things you keep switching on and off such as kettle, toaster, foodmixer.

Make sure that the freezer door closes by itself when left open an inch or so. Most upright freezers have magnets around the door which will close it and keep it closed. But they will not pull the door closed if the freezer tilts forward. Although in general freezers should be installed level, err on the side of tilting it backwards rather than forwards. Tilting backwards by 1° or 2° should not affect the workings.

power cuts and power failure

Power cuts are deliberate actions by the electricity board or someone working there and are usually announced in advance. Power failures are unpremeditated and unpredictable.

If you are given warning that the power will be off, switch on the fast-freeze about 6 hours in advance, to get the maximum cold reserve and put any cold packs you may have into the freezer. Move food with a short storage life to the bottom. Fill in as many spaces as possible with crumpled newspaper: a full freezer will stay cold longer than an almost-empty one when there is no power.

When the power goes off, cover the freezer with a blanket or something similar, to improve the insulation (but do not cover the condenser and pipes on the outside); keep the temperature in the room as low as possible. Treated like this, a chest freezer could keep its contents frozen for up to 48 hours, an upright for about 36 hours.

If power is returned within 24 hours, remove the insulating blanket, leave the fast-freeze switch on (or put it on if you have not already done so). Leave the door or lid closed for a couple more hours. If the power seems likely to be off for more than 24 hours, try and find a friend, or two, who have space in their freezers (assuming of course, they still have power) and transfer the contents.

If you have no warning of a power cut or failure, obviously you cannot build up a reserve of cold. But if you cover the freezer and take the same precautions as for a power cut, the freezer will keep cold for about 30 to 40 hours.

Whatever happens, you must resist the temptation to open the freezer 'to see how things are' or even to remove tonight's dinner. A trip to the fish and chip shop may well prove to be cheaper in the long run.

When power is restored, have a quick look at the contents of the freezer. Packages which are still frozen can be left in the freezer. If thawing has started, a decision has to be made as to what to do with the food:

raw meat, fish and poultry: if they still feel cold, can be cooked and then returned to the freezer

vegetables: can be refrozen after being cooked and used for casseroles or soups, or possibly vegetable purée as a useful addition to many dishes for extra flavour and thickening.

fruit: can generally be refrozen, but on thawing, the fruit will have lost some juice and if refrozen will freeze in one solid mass. This may not matter if the fruit is to be used later in pies or purées. It may be possible to refreeze the larger fruit individually and repack when frozen.

bread, cakes: baked items without cream can be refrozen safely.

icecream and cream: products which contain cream or icecream must not be refrozen, neither should already-prepared meals.

Food which has been subjected to a power cut or failure that lasted longer than 24 hours will not keep as long as the quoted storage times. It is impossible to say how short storage times have become, but it is wise to plan the next month's meals around the freezer contents.

Breakdowns

If the freezer is in a garage or outhouse, the compressor will run infrequently during the winter months, especially during cold snaps. This is nothing to worry about.

A freezer in a garage is more prone to electrical failures caused by moisture, so allow plenty of ventilation around and underneath the freezer, especially if there is also a (wet or snow-covered) car in the garage.

Sometime, sooner or later, something will go wrong with your freezer. (It may even stop working.) If you can find the cause you are in a better position to determine whether a service call is necessary.

calling a service engineer

Before calling a service engineer, make sure that a service call is really necessary and how urgent it is.

You can phone the service department of the manufacturer, but many service departments cannot be contacted in the evening or at weekends (so if your freezer breaks down, for example, early friday evening, most of your food could be ruined before you even ask for an engineer to call).

As an alternative to phoning the manufacturer, you could phone an independent refrigeration engineer, but you run the risk of contacting one of the 'cowboys'. Avoid phoning advertisers who claim to mend virtually everything. It may be best to go by the recommendation of a friend or neighbour. Otherwise, look in your local paper or in yellow pages (see under refrigerator repairs).

When phoning the service engineer, say what the trouble is and tell him the manufacturer, model number and serial number of your freezer so that the right spares can be brought. This information may be in your instruction book but the most reliable source is the rating plate, permanently attached somewhere on or in the freezer (top of the back or on one of the side walls or perhaps hidden by a drawer or basket).

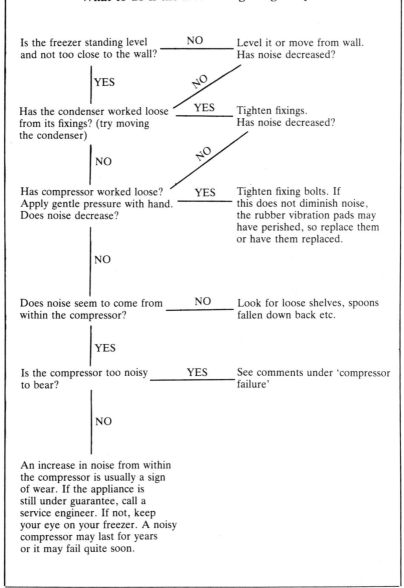

What to do if the freezer is getting noisy

Is the freezer standing level and not too close to the wall?   **NO**   Level it or move from wall. Has noise decreased?

YES

NO

Has the condenser worked loose from its fixings? (try moving the condenser)   **YES**   Tighten fixings. Has noise decreased?

NO

NO

Has compressor worked loose? Apply gentle pressure with hand. Does noise decrease?   **YES**   Tighten fixing bolts. If this does not diminish noise, the rubber vibration pads may have perished, so replace them or have them replaced.

NO

Does noise seem to come from within the compressor?   **NO**   Look for loose shelves, spoons fallen down back etc.

YES

Is the compressor too noisy to bear?   **YES**   See comments under 'compressor failure'

NO

An increase in noise from within the compressor is usually a sign of wear. If the appliance is still under guarantee, call a service engineer. If not, keep your eye on your freezer. A noisy compressor may last for years or it may fail quite soon.

What to do if the mains-on light is not on

Switch to fast-freeze.
Does compressor start?
Does interior light come on
when door is opened?

————— YES —————

The light bulb may have
failed. Replace it (see
instruction book) or have
it replaced.

| NO

Is the plug properly plugged
into socket and switched on?

——— NO ———

Plug in properly, switch on.

| YES

Check the fuse (by replacing it
with either a new one or one from
an appliance which works).
Does the freezer now work?

——— YES ———

One fuse blowing can be
ignored, but if a second
fuse blows within a couple
of months, have the freezer
checked by a service engineer.

| NO

Is there a power cut or failure?
(to check, try the lights in the
house)

——— YES ———

see advice given on p. 68
on action you should take

| NO

Is there power at the socket?
(to check, plug in another
appliance)

——— NO ———

This may be due to poor wiring
behind the socket or maybe a
blown fuse in the fuse box.
Get this checked by a
competent electrician. If
a fuse has blown, you may have
power in another part of the
house (try one on the cooker panel
or upstairs). If not, see advice on
power failure

| YES

Consult service engineer (see p. 70)

What to do if the warning light comes on showing that the freezer is not cold enough

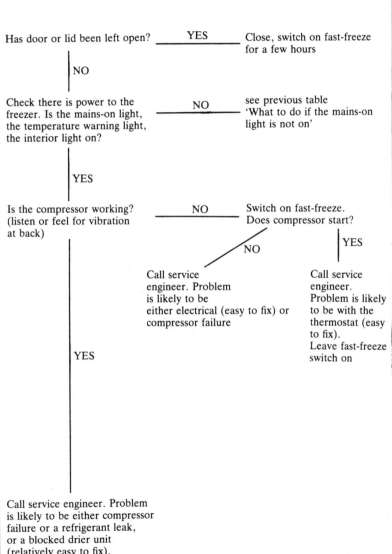

Has door or lid been left open? ————— YES ————— Close, switch on fast-freeze for a few hours

NO

Check there is power to the freezer. Is the mains-on light, the temperature warning light, the interior light on? ————— NO ————— see previous table 'What to do if the mains-on light is not on'

YES

Is the compressor working? (listen or feel for vibration at back) ————— NO ————— Switch on fast-freeze. Does compressor start?

NO

Call service engineer. Problem is likely to be either electrical (easy to fix) or compressor failure

YES

Call service engineer. Problem is likely to be with the thermostat (easy to fix). Leave fast-freeze switch on

YES

Call service engineer. Problem is likely to be either compressor failure or a refrigerant leak, or a blocked drier unit (relatively easy to fix).

What to do if the freezer is getting too cold or the compressor is running continually or ice is building up on the tube coming from inside the freezer at the back

Has the fast-freeze switch been left on accidentally? ————YES———— Switch it off.

|NO

Is the thermostat set up too high (cold)? ————YES———— Turn it to lower setting (but not 'off' or 0). Compressor should switch off if it was running. Check if temperature is still too cold next day.

|NO

Problem is likely to be faulty thermostat. Calling service engineer is likely to be cheaper than cost of extra electricity used, in the long run.

Other symptoms

Water appears under freezer or ice is building up outside freezer (on back or underneath) ———— Insulation is damaged. Some service engineers may replace it but repairs may be less than satisfactory. If the freezer is still under guarantee, and was delivered by the retailer ask for a replacement from the shop where it was bought. If not, keep an eye on temperatures inside freezer, particularly 'warm spots' of less than $-18°C$.

Is there rapid build-up of ice? ————— Check door seal carefully, it may need replacement

replacing the door seal

A door seal can be ordered through your electricity board showroom. You have to know the model number and serial number of your freezer. When it arrives, check that the size of the replacement seal is right.

Look whether the seal on your freezer is fastened by screws or snapped into a groove. To replace a seal that fits into a groove, pull out the old seal carefully, clean the groove and press in the replacement.

If the seal is fastened by screws, they may be the type with an X slot in their head. You must use the appropriate Philips or Posidriv type of screwdriver. First remove all the screws in only the upper half of the door and carefully twist the seal from the plastic inner door and let it hang down. Then fit the new seal on the upper half of the door (start in a corner) and put the screws in but do not tighten them completely.

Remove the screws in the lower half of the door and remove the old seal, then fit the new seal and put in the screws, but do not tighten them completely.

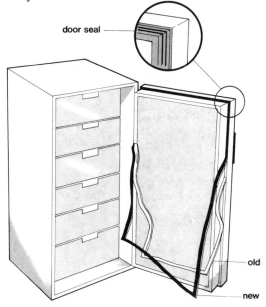

Close the door, make sure the seal is not twisted. Open the door, and tighten the screws. Then check the door sealing with a strip of paper.

Some seals are magnetic on three sides only; the side without magnet (which feels less rigid) should be fitted on the hinge side of the door.

Some seals are moulded to the door and cannot be replaced. A new door would need to be fitted (by a service engineer) if the seal is leaking badly.

compressor failure

Compressors are made in single sealed units and if anything goes wrong, the whole compressor will need to be replaced. It is the most expensive component of the freezer and it may not make economic sense to replace the compressor on a small or old appliance. It may be better to buy a new freezer.

If it is worthwhile to replace the compressor, this should be done with the inside of the freezer at a temperature above freezing. The same applies if there is a refrigerant leak or if the drier unit needs replacing. To replace a compressor, or refrigerant or a drier unit, the engineer must cut into the tubes containing the refrigerant which then escapes into the air (it is harmless). Air then gets inside the refrigerant tubes. Moisture in the air forms droplets of water on cold surfaces and if the surface is cold enough, small crystals of ice will form. If the tubes are below the freezing point of water, small crystals of ice can form within the tubes and could block them.

So if you suspect that
– the compressor may need to be replaced
– the refrigerant may need to be replaced because of a leak
– the drier unit may need to be replaced
try and find a temporary home for your frozen food. If you are shy about asking friends or neighbours, remember that one day they may need to borrow space in yours.

when disposing of an old freezer (or fridge)

Some local authorities have a civic amenity reclamation centre, where you can take unwanted household items, so that they can be disposed of safely and, incidentally, help keep down the rates. If you do not have the necessary transport, you can phone the council who may be able to arrange for the removal of an unwanted large item free, or for a nominal charge.

If your old freezer is still operational but of low or negligible second-hand value, some local voluntary organisation may be able to find it a useful home, as a gift.

If you buy a new freezer, the people who deliver it may be willing to remove the old one and dispose of it. If they seem unwilling, you can try to make it a condition of your buying the new one.

Do not, under any circumstances, dump your rubbish – including a freezer – on verges, in a pond, or layby.

Virtually all freezers and refrigerators on the market today are kept closed by magnetism or the weight of the lid. But many older versions have a catch, which cannot be opened from the inside. During the working life of these appliances, it is extremely unlikely that anything inside should want to get out. But when such an appliance, once finished with, ends up on a rubbish dump somewhere, its boxlike appearance makes it an attractive playhouse. If a child gets inside, he may find that, once shut, the door cannot be opened again, and tragedy would result.

So, if your old freezer or refrigerator has a catch, make sure that you remove it or break it, so that the door cannot be firmly shut; or remove the door altogether. Make sure your rubbish does not hurt other people.

When moving house

A freezer should be the last item to be removed from your old house so that it can be the first to be unloaded and installed in the new one. Make sure you know where it is to go (and that there is the necessary socket there), and tell the removal men where to put it.

– the food

There is a risk that you might damage the freezer by having it moved when it is too heavy. A freezer in relation to its loaded weight is a relatively fragile box and not designed as a transport container. (The exact amount of risk can vary according to the make of freezer). So, ideally, you should run down frozen food stocks before you move, then defrost the freezer and dry it out. Another consideration is that a loaded freezer would be sufficiently heavy to require extra removal men on the job, making the removal significantly more expensive.

If you have to move with frozen food
• try not to take more than a quarter of the capacity of the freezer
• switch on the fast-freeze for at least 24 hours before removal
• do not open the door or the lid of the freezer.

There is a risk that the frozen food will start thawing. Refreezing partially thawed food can spoil its taste and can be a health hazard if the freezer is without current long enough for the food to go off. But do not ask the removal men to plug in the freezer while it is actually loaded on a van, this is not a safe practice.

– the move

During the move, there is the danger of the pipework (with the refrigerant) being squashed or cracked, or the insulation being damaged. Also, an airlock or a blockage can form in the cooling system if the freezer is tipped more than 30°.

Carrying a freezer at an angle is not inevitably going to cause damage – particularly if the tipping angle is away from the drier unit – but damage is likely to occur if it is actually transported in the vehicle at this sort of angle.

Even if a freezer is moved gently and correctly out of the house and onto the removal van, the vibration of the compressor jogging up and down while the van is driving along can fracture the pipes. If the freezer is then switched on, it will not start freezing although the compressor is working. If you then just leave it, it would eventually burn out or seize up (landing you with a hefty bill).

– after the move

This is still not the end of it: during a removal, the vibration while in transit can loosen electrical connections, so after unloading switch on the machine briefly to check that all the lights work.

The removal men may ask you to sign a discharge document, after the move, to confirm that they have completed the job. You should inspect it visually, but may not know until some time later whether the freezer has withstood the journey well.

After removal, a freezer should be left for a period so as to allow the oil in the compressor to settle; allow it to stand for at least two hours. Some furniture removers advise that an even longer period (such as 24 hours) should be allowed to elapse before the freezer is permanently switched on again.

On the whole, it may be a good idea to consider selling your freezer with the house, and either buy a new one or buy the one left as a fixture by the seller of your new house.

Food for the freezer

Although a freezer is most money-saving when you use it to freeze
what you yourself have cooked (or what somebody else has given you),
it is most time-saving when you buy ready-frozen.

buying ready-frozen food

Whether you buy from your local supermarket or a specialised freezer
centre, there are several things you should bear in mind.

- Do not go shopping for frozen food on a hot day, if it can be avoided.
  The food in the shop is likely to be warmer than −18°C, particularly
  if it is in a lidded freezer, because the air which enters the freezer
  each time it is opened is very warm. Also, there is always inevitably
  a short delay between taking a package from the shop's freezer and
  placing it in your own, time in which the food can start to thaw. So,
  during hot weather, shop early in the day.
- Switch on your fast-freeze switch before you go out or even a couple
  of hours earlier.
- Take with you a thick paper bag or newspaper, or a coldbox if you
  have one.
- Buy your frozen food last, after you have done the rest of your
  shopping (including any window-shopping). In a supermarket, get
  the dry and tinned goods first and select any frozen goods immediately before going to the checkout.
- Avoid shopping at busy times when you may have to queue at the
  checkout: midweek is generally better than at the weekend.
- Choose carefully. Some shop freezers have thermometers: the reading should be at least −18°C. Many commercial freezers have a load
  line. Goods should not be stocked above this line (but often are).
  This may be the fault of a customer who, in looking for just the
  joint the size she wants, inadvertently piled the remainder above
  the load line. (Make sure that when you go digging for that elusive
  joint you do not pile the remainder too high.) It can also be the
  fault of the shop where the assistants have not been properly trained
  and have overloaded the freezers. Avoid buying from an overloaded
  freezer, but do report it to the manager.
- In a freezer centre which has lidded chest freezers, avoid buying

from one with excessive build-up of frost along the top, or one where the lid does not close properly.

- Beware of packages which feel damp. If the package has been stored correctly it should not feel damp. Make sure that there are no splits or holes in the packaging which could result in freezer burn. Where you can do so, examine any frozen food for freezer burn.
- Some types of plastic tub develop splits when stored in a freezer, so look carefully before you buy – it is too late if you notice it only after you get home.
- Avoid packages with a lot of frost inside; it could mean the package is old.

If everything is not as you would wish, mention it to the store manager. There is not a great deal of choice in freezer centres, and it is in your interest, and that of other freezer owners in your neighbourhood, to ensure that the local freezer centre is up to scratch.

When you have chosen, wrap the frozen food well in the newspaper or thick paper sacks (or put some of it into the coldbox). Take the food straight home and put it straight into the freezer. Leave the fast-freeze switch on for a couple more hours.

Most prepared foods bought ready-frozen have a short storage life, 3 months or less, marked on it. This is because the manufacturers want to ensure that you eat their product at its best, and to encourage you to eat it sooner rather than later, so that you will go out and buy some more. Also, they cannot be sure how well the produce has been stored between initial freezing and arriving at the customer's freezer.

ready-frozen v. bulk buying

Buying a sack of peas, particularly at their 'glut' prices, is cheaper than buying one pound. Buying peas by the field is even cheaper. That is what the commercial companies do, and freeze them within a couple of hours of picking, whereas 'fresh' at the greengrocers usually means 2 days old, or older.

Visiting a 'pick-your-own' farm can be an excellent idea – often combining cheapness with freshness. A special visit to a 'pick-your-own' farm can, however, take a lot of petrol compared with a visit to the frozen food section while you are already at the supermarket. And if you do actually have to pick your own, rather than buy from the farm shop, the picking can be tedious, time-consuming and back-breaking. In some places, 'pick-your-own' farming has become big business , so check the prices at the local greengrocers before you go. You may be tempted to buy more than you intended (and the children may demand ice-creams). The main advantage is the freshness of the produce and the fact that you are unlikely to have to discard rotten fruit.

When comparing the prices, bear in mind the quantity of fresh vegetables you must buy, stalks, pods, and all, on average, to yield 100 g (about a quarter of a pound) ready for use – that is, similar to commercially frozen vegetables.

To get 100 grammes brussels sprouts you need 125 g
To get 100 grammes carrots you need 120 g
To get 100 grammes cauliflower you need 160 g
To get 100 grammes celery (stick) you need 135 g
To get 100 grammes green beans you need 110 g
To get 100 grammes leeks you need 175 g
To get 100 grammes peas, you need 250 g
To get 100 grammes savoy cabbage, you need 140 g
To get 100 grammes white cabbage, you need 130 g.

And remember that a sackful of peas can take an awful long time to shell and prepare for freezing. Home freezing can be fun but do not go overboard and buy a hundredweight just because it seems a bargain.

Suitability for freezing:
*** best
** quite good
* not very good
– do not freeze

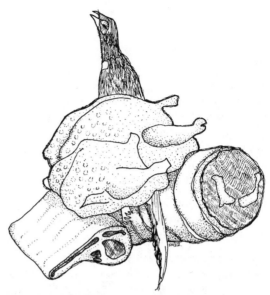

Meat

Owning a freezer may mean reorganising one's thoughts about the food budget. After spending £50 or more on meat for the freezer, it is only too easy to forget, when doing the weekly shopping, that the meat money has already been spent and that you do not really have an extra couple of pounds to spend on luxuries you might not otherwise have thought of buying. Also, it is going to cost at least as much to replace the meat when it is used up – quite apart from the fact that you may eat more meat, simply because it is there.

One needs to be quite realistic and strong-minded about this, perhaps actually putting aside a sum of money each week or month so that the cash is available when the next large purchase is due.

buying

The obvious place to buy meat is from the butcher, but you can buy meat in bulk, either fresh or frozen, from a feezer centre, cash and carry store, supermarket or farm shop. The advantage of buying from your regular butcher is that he can cut the meat and pack it to individual requirements and is able to take into account your personal preferences – and give advice as well. (But if you have a good local butcher, there may be no point in occupying freezer space with large quantities of meat rather than store just a standby of small quantities of, say, minced beef, chops, sausages, sausage meat.)

buying fresh meat

The advantage of buying fresh meat is that you can decide whether you want the meat on or off the bone. Remember that meat on the bone takes up roughly twice as much space as boneless meat. You can buy part of a carcase, single cuts or a selection of mixed cuts. You can ask your supplier to cut the meat into the size and type you most often use for cooking. The meat will be cut and packed and the supplier might freeze it for you.

Remember when buying 'fresh' meat for the freezer, it is likely to have been frozen and thawed already. New Zealand lamb is usually frozen for transport to this country, and so is most beef from South America.

It is worth matching your purchase to the sort of meat dishes you most frequently prepare. When you buy a whole or part of a carcase, you get a variety of cuts which, depending on the type of meat, provide varying proportions of roasting, stewing and braising meat and/or mince, chops and steaks. The price you pay per pound is less than it would be if you bought a smaller quantity of one cut of meat, but you are getting bones and cheaper cuts, too. With beef, you generally buy a whole forequarter or whole hindquarter. The forequarter has more meat for braising; the hindquarter more meat for roasting and should contain one kidney. Families who like only roasts and grills would not be happy with the mainly braising and stewing cuts from a forequarter of beef.

Freezing the meat yourself can take quite a long time because you should never freeze more than 20 per cent of the contents of the freezer in one day. With a 5 cu ft freezer, you can freeze 1 cu ft per day, equivalent to about 30 lbs of meat. So, freezing a bulk load can take two or three days and it is important to keep the meat chilled in the refrigerator meanwhile, or to arrange to collect the meat in batches from the butcher's cold store.

Prepare the freezer by switching to fast-freeze at least 2 hours before the meat arrives. First freeze offal, mince and cut-up meat; freeze the largest pieces of meat last. Trim any excess fat from the meat: it wastes freezer space and also shortens freezer life (fat eventually turns rancid even in a low temperature).

Remember to switch the control back to 'normal' about 12 hours after the last batch of meat goes into the freezer.

What a freezer will hold

animal	approximate quantity		freezer space needed
Beef hindquarter			
Average gross weight	155 lb	(70 kg)	4 cu ft
Total usable meat (boneless)	107 lb	(48 kg)	(114 litres)
Roasting joints	63 lb	(28 kg)	
Grilling steaks	16 lb	(7 kg)	
Meat for stews and mince	26 lb	(12 kg)	
Kidney	2 lb	(1 kg)	
Beef forequarter			
Average gross weight	145 lb	(66 kg)	3½ cu ft
Total usable meat (boneless)	101 lb	(45 kg)	(99 litres)
Roasting joints	12 lb	(5 kg)	
Braising steaks and joints	60 lb	(27 kg)	
Meat for stews and mince	29 lb	(13 kg)	
Whole lamb			
Average gross weight	35 lb	(16 kg)	1½ cu ft
Total usable meat	32 lb	(14¼ kg)	(43 litres)
Roasting joints (with bone)	18 lb	(8 kg)	
Grills chops (with bone)	9 lb	(4 kg)	
Stewing meat (with bone)	4½ lb	(2 kg)	
Kidney	½ lb	(¼ kg)	
Side of pork			
Average gross weight	50 lb	(23 kg)	2 cu ft
Total usable meat	46 lb	(21 kg)	(57 litres)
Roasting joints (with bone)	27 lb	(12 kg)	
Grills, chops	13 lb	(6 kg)	
Head and trotters	6 lb	(3 kg)	

1 kg = 2.20 lb	1 cu ft = 28.32 litres
1 lb = 0.453 kg	1 litre = 0.35 cu ft

buying frozen meat

Ready-frozen meat can be bought, cut and packaged, from freezer centres, specialist suppliers, cash and carry stores, supermarkets and from some butchers. When buying ready-frozen meat, the labelling might be insufficient, or even wrong ('chops' without specifying the amount or type). Also, there is a risk, if you have ordered a large quantity of meat (perhaps a jointed carcase), that an unscrupulous dealer might sell you more of the cheaper cuts and fewer expensive ones than the animal actually possesses.

Instead of buying a large piece of any animal, you could buy a bulk pack either of a mixed-bag of joints (some butchers will prepare these to your requirements) or of one particular type of joint, which is sometimes offered at a discount.

A carcase is cheaper, but not if you get left with a lot of unwanted cuts. One way of taking advantage of the possible cash saving, without having too much meat, is for several households to share a bulk buy. For instance, two families can share a pig, each having one complete side.

A recent development is 'free flow' meat: cubes of meat or sticks of mince individually frozen before packaging. The advantages are that the housewife can use as much or as little as she needs and the meat can be cooked straight from frozen. (That means no more trying to estimate what sizes are going to be needed, and no more need to allow time to thaw, before the meat can be cut up.)

look out for

When buying frozen meat, look for good packaging so that you know the meat has been well protected. Avoid
- torn packs – unhygienic, and may lead to freezer burn, that is dehydration causing patches where the texture and taste of the meat may have been affected
- excessive drip which shows up as frozen blood inside the pack; this may mean that the meat has been frozen too slowly or stored at too high a temperature
- very dark colour; beef goes very dark when frozen, but if it looks almost black, this may mean that the meat has dried out during storage

- a lot of frost on the surface of the meat; this may mean that the meat has been kept too long or has been thawed and refrozen or that the packaging is inadequate.

warning!

Although frozen meat that has been taken out of the freezer, thawed and cooked, can be put into the freezer again for refreezing in its new form, what you should not do is to refreeze meat in the same (uncooked) form. For example, frozen steak can be made into a casserole and refrozen, or frozen mince can be thawed, made into shepherds pie and then frozen again in this form. But if you buy 'fresh' (that is not frozen) New Zealand lamb chops, which are likely to have been frozen for transport, do not put them in the freezer unless you have cooked them first.

thawing or cooking from frozen?

Raw joints of frozen meat should be thawed slowly in a refrigerator, allowing at least 5 to 6 hours per lb. This means that a 4 lb joint for sunday lunch should be put into the fridge on saturday morning. Thawing times are shorter if the joint is left at room temperature (allow about 2 hours per lb, and keep the meat well wrapped). Thawing at room temperature is not recommended for pork or for large pieces of any meat.

Small joints of meat (but not boned or rolled) can be cooked straight from the freezer. This may make the meat tougher or less juicy; try cooking straight from frozen and compare with thawed-first meat. To cook from frozen takes longer (and therefore costs more). Cooking times depend on the size of joint. Here is an approximate guide.

Roasting from frozen (at 180°C, 350°F, gas mark 4)

joint under 4 lb	cooking time per pound
beef or lamb well done	35 minutes per lb, plus 35 minutes
beef medium or rare	30 minutes per lb, plus 30 minutes
pork well done	45 minutes per lb, plus 45 minutes

A meat thermometer helps to make sure that the joint is thoroughly cooked. When you think the meat should be ready, insert the thermometer; typical readings are:

beef
rare	65°C(150°F)
medium	70°C(160°F)
well done	80°C(170°F)

lamb   80°C(170°F)

pork   80°C(170°F)

– steak and chops

Thawing times for steaks and chops depend on the thickness. In general allow:
up to ½ in thick 5 hrs (refrigerator), 2 hrs (room temp)
up to 1 in thick 8 hrs (refrigerator), 2–3 hrs (room temp)
over 1 in thick 8–10 hrs (refrigerator), 3–4 hrs (room temp).
Thawing at room temperature is not recommended for pork.

Steak and chops can also be cooked straight from frozen, but this may make them tougher. Fry or grill the steak on a high setting until slightly browned on each side, then reduce the heat, turning the meat frequently to keep the surfaces moist and evenly cooked. As a rough guide, you should allow twice the cooking time of fresh cuts.

– in a microwave oven

Joints can be successfully thawed in a microwave oven with a defrost setting. Make sure that you follow the sequence of on and off times indicated with your microwave oven instructions; for instance for 5 lb loin of pork it may be 10 minutes on, 20 minutes off, 5 minutes on, 20 minutes off (with the '5 minutes on, 20 minutes off' repeated, if necessary.)

To ensure even penetration of waves during cooking, turn and rotate the meat frequently. Protect the thinner parts of the roasts (for instance of a leg of lamb) with foil not only during thawing but also during the first part of cooking.

Steaks and sausages should be separated out and thawed in a single layer.

meat

meat	how suitable for freezing	preparation for freezing	storage time	thawing time at room temperature	in refrigerator
				if possible thaw all meat in refrigerator	
beef joints	***	make sure joints are a usable size; wipe with clean damp cloth or kitchen paper, cut off excess fat. Pad any protruding bones to prevent tearing the wrapping. Wrap well in foil or polythene; overwrap	12 months	*under 4 lb* 1–2 hr/lb *over 4 lb* 2–3 hr/lb	*under 4 lb* 3–4 hr/lb *over 4 lb* 4–7 hr/lb
mince	***	if making your own, use very fresh meat, discard as much fat as possible, pack in foil or polythene in usable quantities (e.g. 1 lb)	3 months	2–3 hr/lb	4–7 hr/lb
steak	***	wipe with clean damp cloth or kitchen paper, cut off excess fat. Wrap individually, or separate steaks with foil, film or waxed paper; overwrap	6 months	2–3 hr	5–6 hr
stewing	***	cut into pieces and pack in polythene bags, remove as much air as possible from bags	6 months	2–4 hr	5–6 hr
lamb joints	***	wipe meat with a clean damp cloth or kitchen paper, cut off excess fat; pad any protruding bones to prevent tearing the wrapping, wrap well in foil or polythene, overwrap	8 months	*under 3 lb* 1–2 hr/lb *over 3 lb* 2–3 hr/lb	*under 3 lb* 3–4 hr/lb *over 3 lb* 4–7 hr/lb
chops	***	wipe with clean damp cloth or kitchen paper, remove excess fat; wrap individually or separate chops with foil, film or waxed paper; overwrap	8 months	2–4 hr	5–6 hr
stewing	***	cut into pieces and pack in polythene bags, remove as much air as possible from bags	6 months	2–4 hr	5–6 hr

meat	how suitable for freezing	preparation for freezing	storage time	thawing time at room temperature	in refrigerator
					if possible thaw in fridge
pork joints	***	wipe with clean damp cloth or kitchen paper; remove excess fat; pad any protruding bones to prevent tearing wrapping; wrap well in foil or polythene; overwrap	6 months	under 3 lb 1–2 hr/lb over 3 lb 2–3 hr/lb	under 3 lb 3–4 hr/lb over 3 lb 4–7 hr/lb
chops	***	wipe with clean damp cloth or kitchen paper; remove excess fat; wrap individually, or separate chops with foil, film or waxed paper; overwrap	4 months	1 in thick chops or cutlets 2–4 hr	5–6 hr
salted or pickled	—	do not freeze			
bacon rashers	*	overwrap vacuum packs with heavy polythene	3 months	2–3 hr	4–6 hr
veal joints	***	make sure joints are a usable size; wipe with clean damp cloth or kitchen paper, cut off excess fat; pad any protruding bones to prevent tearing the wrapping; wrap well in foil or polythene; overwrap	6 months	3 hr/lb	5–6 hr/lb
chops	***	wipe with clean damp cloth or kitchen paper, cut off excess fat; wrap individually or separate chops with foil, film or waxed paper; overwrap	4 months	2–4 hr	5–6 hr
offal (heart, kidney, liver, tongue)	*	highly perishable, so better bought already-frozen	3–4 months		6–8 hr/lb
tripe	*	slice, or leave whole	2 months	3–4 hr	6–8 hr/lb

Poultry

Poultry should be completely thawed before cooking, preferably in a refrigerator. Thawing out in water tends to leave the bird dry and tasteless.

The bigger the frozen bird, the longer it will take to thaw. A large turkey can take several days to thaw properly, so you should allow for this when planning a meal. Thawing should be done in a cool place, otherwise there is a chance that the outside will spoil before the inside is properly thawed.

If you have a whole frozen bird and need portions for a recipe, joint and cut up the frozen bird, then thaw the individual pieces. This is quicker than thawing out the whole bird and then jointing it.

the danger of food poisoning

Poultry is one of the commonest sources of salmonella. Salmonella are killed by heat, but if the heat is not sufficient, the bacteria will increase and can cause food poisoning. Poultry should not be eaten under-cooked.

Poultry can also be the indirect cause of food poisoning by contaminating other foods which are then eaten without further cooking. It is, therefore, important that strict hygiene precautions should be followed when storing or handling uncooked poultry. When thawing frozen poultry, take special care that the water which drips out does not contaminate other food or work surfaces. Do not prepare poultry near cooked foods; wash all knives, cloths and work surfaces thoroughly immediately after use.

Always cook poultry thoroughly so that none of the flesh remains pink.

stuffed poultry

It takes a long time for the cold to penetrate into the centre of a stuffed bird, and as stuffings tend to have a short freezer life, it is not recommended to freeze a stuffed bird. Freeze poultry and stuffing separately. Stuffing does not keep as long, and also prevents quick freezing.

Game for freezing must be hung before it is frozen and not after it has thawed out.

poultry and game

type	how suitable for freezing	how to prepare for freezing	storage time	thawing time	notes
chicken	***	wipe inside and out with clean damp cloth; tie legs and wings to body, and pad to prevent their tearing the wrapping; wrap well in foil or polythene freeze giblets separately	1 year giblets 2 months	medium size chicken in fridge 24 hr; or overnight at cool room temperature	*do not freeze stuffed; thaw wrapped*
duck	***	as for chicken	6 months giblets 2 months	in fridge 24 hr or 12–15 hr at room temperature	*thaw wrapped; use older birds for casseroles or pies*
goose	***	as for chicken	4 months giblets 2 months	in fridge 24–36 hr or 16–20 hr at room temperature	*thaw wrapped; has a short storage life because it is so fatty*
grouse	***	should be hung before freezing; then prepare as for chicken	6 months	in fridge 5 hr/lb	*use older birds for casseroles or pies*
hare	***	skin and draw; wipe inside and out with clean damp cloth but do not wash; wrap well in foil or polythene	6 months	in fridge 5 hr/lb	*roast back (saddle) and legs; remainder can be braised*
partridge	***	as for grouse	6 months	in fridge 5 hr/lb	*do not thaw in pear tree*
pheasant	***	as for grouse	6 months	in fridge 5 hr/lb	

pigeon	***	pluck and draw, then prepare as for chicken; can be frozen casseroled	6 months	in fridge 5 hr/lb or 3–6 hr at room temperature	*if casserole, gently heat from frozen*
plover	***	pluck and singe but do not draw; cut off head and neck; pack in polythene bag	6 months	in fridge 5 hr/lb or 3–6 hr at room temperature	
quail	***	as for plover	6 months	in fridge 5 hr/lb	
rabbit	***	skin and draw, cut into joints; pack in polythene bag	10 months	in fridge 5 hr/lb	*freeze only when absolutely fresh*
turkey	***	as for chicken (but most turkeys are too large to freeze satisfactorily in a domestic freezer and take a very long time to thaw)	6 months	24–36 hr at cool room temperature, or in fridge 40–60 hr	*may affect contents of refrigerator when thawing*
venison	***	must be well-hung before freezing; wipe well with clean damp cloth; wrap joints well in foil or polythene; overwrap	8 months	in fridge 5 hr/lb	*thawing in marinade makes it less dry*
woodcock	***	as for plover	6 months	in fridge 5 hr/lb	

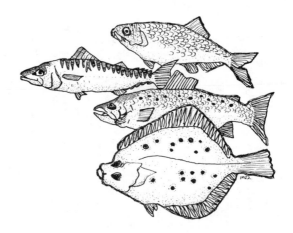

Fish

Fish is at its best only when really fresh, and therefore should be frozen as soon as possible after it is caught. If you buy from a fishmonger, try to buy whole fish with bright colours and clear, bright eyes, red gills and firm flesh. That dull opaque look in the eye is a sure sign of stale fish. Do not buy unless you are sure it is fresh and that it has not been previously frozen – a rare combination with provincial fishmongers these days.

In many parts of the country it is difficult to buy fresh fish. But a day-trip to the seaside might be rewarding if you go properly prepared. Also there are fish farms in various parts of the country, where you can buy fresh trout and other fish for your freezer.

Before freezing fish, it is a good rule to gut it and remove the tail and fins with a sharp knife, wash well and drain; do not remove the skin; cut large fish into steaks or fillets.

Lobsters, shrimps and prawns are generally already cooked when you buy them (you can tell by the colour). If not, they should be cooked before freezing: put them into water that has just boiled, bring back to the boil and continue boiling for about 15 minutes. Oysters and scallops can be frozen raw.

Dry pack: wrap the fish completely in foil or film, making sure that all air is excluded, overwrap and seal.

Acid pack: citric acid preserves the flavour and colour of fish because it prevents the fats combining with oxygen in air and becoming rancid. Citric acid powder is readily available from chemists (often with the wine making equipment). Dip fish into a solution of 1 part citric acid to 100 parts water, drain wrap and seal.

Glazing: this process is best used for whole fish, salmon for example. First wash and gut the fish and then place, in a dish, in the coldest part of the freezer, close to the evaporator. When the fish is frozen solid – 2 to 3 hours depending on the size of the fish – remove from the freezer and dip into very cold water so that a thin coating of ice will form. Return to the freezer for approximately an hour and then repeat the dipping. After 4 or 5 dips, the ice coating should have built up to about ¼ in. The glazed fish should then be wrapped in foil or film.

If you want to remove the skin from frozen fillets of fish, run each fillet under the tap for a couple of minutes, letting the water flow across the skin. By bending the top of the fillet (about ⅛ in from the top) and pulling downwards, the skin can be peeled off the frozen fish.

However, this method of removing skin can rip away the flesh, especially on flat fish and thin fillets, so it is best used for larger fish fillets of cod or haddock.

fish

fish	preparation for freezing (after basic cleaning etc)	storage time	thawing time
bloater	wrap carefully and well, then overwrap at least once (otherwise strong smell may be absorbed by other foods)	2 months	overnight in fridge or 3 hr at room temperature
cod	wrap well and ensure that air is excluded (or fish will be dry and tasteless); overwrap	3 months	6–10 hr/lb in fridge 3–5 hr/lb at room temperature cook small pieces from frozen
cod roe	cut into half-inch slices and pack in rigid container with paper between the slices	1 month	dust with flour and fry from frozen
coley	as for cod	3 months	as for cod
crab (only if absolutely fresh)	must be cooked; remove edible meat from shells; pack in rigid containers; or arrange in cleaned crab shells and wrap	1 month	6–8 hr in fridge
crayfish	(to gut, pull to remove central portion of the fan-shaped tail bringing the intestinal tube with it) cook in boiling water for 10 minutes, cool and pack in polythene bag	2–3 months	6–8 hr in fridge
eel, fresh	divide into portions, wrap well	1–2 months	cook from frozen or partly thawed
eel, smoked	freeze only if freshly smoked	1–2 months	4–5 hr in package in fridge 2 hr at room temperature (keep packed)
haddock fresh or smoked	as for cod	3 months	as for cod

herring	head and tail can be left on, wash, wrap well to exclude all air	2 months	cook from frozen
kippers	wrap carefully and well, then overwrap (so that strong smell is not absorbed by other foods)	2 months	cook from frozen
lobster	freeze on same day as caught; must be boiled; cool then wrap well, or remove meat after cooking and pack in rigid container or polythene bag	1 month	6–8 hr in fridge
mackerel	can be frozen ungutted; wash, wrap well	2 months	3–4 hr in fridge 1½–2 hr at room temperature
mussels	discard any with broken shells or which will not shut tightly. Wash and scrub well. Place in large saucepan with a little wine or water; cook covered, on medium heat for 3 minutes – until they open; discard any unopened ones; cool, pack with or without shells in rigid container or polythene bag with their own juice	1 month	overnight in fridge
oysters	open carefully and retain juice, pack in rigid container with juice	1 month	6–8 hr in fridge or cook from frozen in soup or sauce; do not boil
plaice	as for cod	3 months	as for cod
prawns	if bought uncooked, wash thoroughly, boil in lightly salted water for 2–4 minutes; shell and pack in rigid container; or can be frozen in shells	2 months	1 hr in fridge
salmon	as for cod	3 months	as for cod

fish	preparation for freezing (after basic cleaning etc)	storage time	thawing time
scallops	scrub well, place in hot oven and remove as soon as shells start to open (if left until completely open, flesh could be cooked); take off black fringe; cut away from shell; wash in salted water; pack in rigid container	1 month	cook from frozen or thaw overnight in fridge
sprats	rinse well and open-freeze on a tray	2 months	1 hr in fridge. Do not deep-fry from frozen (fat would spit)
shrimps	as for prawns	2 months	as for prawns
sole	as for cod	3 months	as for cod
trout	gut, remove head, tail and fins; wash well, wrap each fish carefully to exclude air, overwrap	2 months	cook from frozen or 4–6 hr in fridge, 2–3 hr at room temperature
turbot	as for cod	3 months	as for cod
whitebait	as for sprats	2 months	as for sprats
whiting	as for cod	3 months	as for cod

Bread cakes and pastry

In storing cakes, pastry and bread, the freezer shows one of its great advantages: the convenience of taking a cake out of the cupboard and the luxury of that fresh-from-the-oven taste.

Making bread is a time-consuming task which, if bread is to be eaten fresh, has to be done at least once a week. But if there is room in the freezer to store the loaves, bread-making need only be done once a month or so; it depends how many friends and relatives will want to eat this bread (and, on the whole, if people make their own bread, more gets eaten). It may not be a practical proposition, bearing in mind the quantities required to provide bread for four weeks for a family – lugging all that flour home, the volume of rising dough, even if mixing and kneading have been done in manageable quantities, and the marathon baking session. But even if you do not bake your own, the freezer can be very useful for keeping bread.

If members of your family take sandwiches for lunch, it is easier to make a batch of sandwiches at a time, wrap them individually and freeze. Put into a rigid container or large polythene bag and label with the type of filling. If sandwiches are removed from the freezer before leaving for school or work, they will thaw in the lunch box (and help to keep the other contents cool). It saves the last-minute rush in the morning and cries of 'not cheese again'.

Cakes are a useful standby. A whole sandwich cake takes an hour or two to thaw but, at a pinch, when your mother-in-law is on the doorstep, pop the cake in the oven (200°F, gas mark ¼ or low) for a few minutes. Butter-cream fillings freeze well, but jam tends to seep into the cake. Sandwich cakes thaw more quickly if they are frozen unfilled; fill and dust with sugar when thawed. Small cakes and scones thaw in about half an hour. Unbaked scones, open-frozen and then stored in polythene bags, will thaw while an oven heats to baking temperatures and can then be served fresh-baked.

Baked goods that were frozen and then reheated tend to go stale more quickly than fresh items.

Fruit cakes and tea-loaves can be sliced and interleaved before freezing, and individual slices then removed and thawed as required.

baked things

baked things	how suitable for freezing	how to prepare for freezing	storage time	thawing time	notes
biscuits	**	allow freshly-baked biscuits to cool; wrap in foil or polythene can also be open-frozen unbaked; then place in rigid container or wrap roll of dough in heavy-duty foil	6 months	½–3 hr at room temperature	*uncooked rolls of dough should be thawed slightly then sliced; uncooked shaped biscuits can be baked direct from frozen; allow extra 5 min*
bread	***	leave bought bread in original wrapper, then overwrap wrap home-made bread in foil or polythene bag	1 month	3–6 hr at room temperature or in fridge overnight	*sliced bread can be toasted from frozen*
– crusty loaf (vienna, french) whole	***	wrap in foil	1 week	3 hr at room temperature	*crisp up in hot oven for up to 5 minutes before serving*
– leftover	***	cut into chunks, put into polythene bags	1 month	½–2 hr at room temperature	*put on a plate and cover with foil to prevent drying out, place in hot oven for about 5 minutes, or steam loosely wrapped in foil*
– dough (unrisen)	***	wrap in lightly greased polythene bags or foil in usable quantities, seal well	4 months	5–6 hr at room temperature or in fridge overnight	*unseal bag for thawing; let rise, then shape and bake*

Item	Rating	Preparation / wrapping	Storage	Thawing	Notes
– sandwiches	**	spread with butter or margarine to prevent the filling from soaking into the bread; interleave; wrap in foil or polythene; overwrap	1 month	2–3 hr in wrapping	*do not use fillings of hard boiled eggs, salad vegetables, salad cream, tomato, bananas; season sparingly*
cakes – uniced	***	interleave the 2 halves of sandwich cakes (or flan cases) with foil or waxed paper, overwrap with polythene and pack in rigid container; fillings and decorations can be frozen separately	6 months	1½–2 hr	*add any icing or filling after thawing*
– griddle/drop scones	***	interleave; wrap in polythene bag	1 month	1 hr	*thaw in kitchen paper or tea-towel*
– scones	**	wrap in polythene bag; can also be open-frozen unbaked	6 months	1 hr	*reheat from frozen, wrapped in foil at 200°C (400°F) for 10 minutes*
choux pastry (cooked)	***	bake, fill and decorate, then open-freeze; when frozen, pack in polythene bag or rigid container	3 months	2 hr unwrap to thaw	*if filling is cream (for instance in eclairs) fill after thawing*
croissants, danish pastries (unbaked)	***	prepare as far as adding all the fat, but do not roll out, wrap in large polythene bags	6 weeks	5 hr or overnight in fridge	*unseal bag, leave dough in it to rise, then proceed to baking*
(baked)	***	wrap in polythene bags	4 weeks	5 hr	*reheat for about 4 min or reheat from frozen in foil for 15 min*

baked things

baked things	how suitable for freezing	how to prepare for freezing	storage time	thawing time	notes
doughnuts	***	let cool; pack without sugar or icing	1–2 months		*heat up from frozen for 15 minutes at 200°C (400°F)*
macaroons	—	do not freeze			*they become sticky*
mince pies	***	open-freeze uncooked, in the tins; do not glaze or make holes in tops of pies; when frozen store in rigid containers	3–6 months	2 hr	*return to original tins, make vents in tops of pies and glaze after thawing bake at 220°C (425°F) 20–30 min*
pastry (unbaked shortcrust)	***	can be frozen in blocks, rolled into shapes or made into complete dishes in foil containers; open-freeze; when hard wrap in polythene bags	6 months	1–3 hr depending on amount	*little advantage in bulk freezing shortcrust as it takes 3 hr to thaw*
flaky, puffed	***	prepare pastry to the last rolling, wrap in bags or foil and overwrap, open-freeze pastry shapes and stack with foil or wax paper in between	6 months	3–4 hr	*can be filled while frozen; put unbaked pie shells or flan cases into original containers before baking from frozen. Add 5 minutes to normal baking time*
(baked)	***	let cool; open-freeze, wrap carefully (because fragile) or put in foil containers	6 months	2–4 hr	*allow flan cases to thaw before adding fruit; can be heated up but do not rebake*

rolls, (baked) ***	open-freeze, then pack in polythene bags	4–6 months	in packaging, 1½ hr room temperature	*heat from frozen, wrapped in foil 15 min (hot oven)*
(part baked) ***	open-freeze, then pack in polythene bags	2–4 months		*bake from frozen at 220°C (425°F) for 15 minutes*
spongecake ***	wrap whole or in slices	3–6 months depending on filling	1 hr slices (wrapped) 4–6 hr whole	
teabreads ***	wrap in polythene bag whole or in interleaved slices	3 months	½ hr if sliced	*remove only as many slices as required*
yeast (fresh) –	make sure it is really fresh, not crumbly; wrap in 1 oz portions in foil or polythene	1 month	½ hr at room temperature	*can go watery on thawing; would keep in refrigerator 3–4 weeks if well sealed*

Suitability for freezing: *** best, ** quite good, * not very good, – do not freeze

Dairy produce

On the whole, dairy produce is so generally and easily available, without seasonal variation in price, that it is not a top priority for freezing. But it is useful to store some butter and margarine against running out, and cream as a stand-by. Freezing cream is not easy; the higher the fat content, the better for freezing. Whipping cream or double cream is best if chilled and then semi-whipped before freezing. A little sugar added seems to prevent the cream from separating.

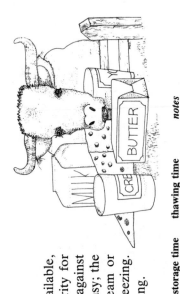

dairy produce	how suitable for freezing	how to prepare for freezing	storage time	thawing time	notes
butter	***	overwrap	unsalted 6 months salted 3 months	in fridge overnight or 1–2hr at room temperature	
cheese (eg Cheddar, Cheshire, Double Glos, Edam, Gouda)	**	divide into usable portions, wrap well to prevent drying out	6 months	in fridge overnight or 1–2hr at room temperature	*cheese does not mature after freezing; also it becomes more crumbly*
(eg Camembert, Port Salut, Stilton, Danish Blue, Roquefort)	*	divide into usable portions, wrap well to prevent drying out and cross contamination	3 months	in fridge overnight	
cottage cheese	–				*does not freeze well*
cream cheese	*	freeze quickly in rigid container	6 weeks	in fridge overnight	*becomes yellow and hard after long storage*

cream (fresh)	—				*does not freeze well (but ready-frozen can be bought)*
eggs	***	do not freeze in shell remove from shells, stir to blend whites and yolks; add ½ teaspoon salt or sugar per six eggs to prevent thickening	6 months	40 minutes at room temperature	*3 tablespoons mixed whole egg = 1 whole egg*
eggs (hard boiled)	—				*not suitable for freezing*
egg – yolk	**	mix with a little salt or sugar; pack in rigid container or ice-cube trays	6 months	1 hr at room temperature	*1 tablespoon yolk = 1 egg yolk*
egg – white	***	whisk lightly, pack in rigid containers	6 months	1 hr at room temperature	*2 tablespoons white = 1 egg white*
margarine	***	overwrap	3 months	in fridge 5–8 hr or 1–2 hr at room temperature	
milk (homogenised)	*	freeze only in cartons: milk bottles are likely to crack	1 month	in fridge overnight or 5–8 hr at room temperature	*pasteurised milk does not freeze well because the fat separates*
yogurt (low-fat)	—				*liable to separate; but ready-frozen yogurt can be bought*

Fruit

Fruit should be frozen as soon as possible after picking. Where it is necessary to wash the fruit, put it in a collander and dip briefly into very cold water. Handle gently to avoid bruising.

Do not freeze bruised or damaged or unsound fruit, but misshapen fruit may be pulped or puréed before freezing, for use in desserts. Very ripe fruit, too, should be frozen as purée.

Fruit may be frozen dry without or with sugar, free flow (open-frozen); in a syrup; or as a purée.

dry, without sugar

If you have washed the fruit, dry it and pack in rigid containers. Alternatively, open-freeze the fruit by laying it individually on a tray (baking trays are useful for this, or you can use a sheet of foil instead of a tray), and place in the freezer. This process is also known as 'free-flow freezing'. Once solid, the fruit can be removed and packed in polythene bags or plastic containers and as much or as little as is wanted can be removed.

A useful idea is to save the trays from boxes of chocolates (if anyone gives you this sort of chocolates). Fruits or berries can be placed individually in the little wells and the whole lot stuck on the baking tray for open-freezing. This is less trouble than lining them all separately on the tray and having them roll about when loading into the freezer. They can be removed quite easily from the chocolate box tray for putting into polythene bags.

If you want to open-freeze more than one layer, separate the baking trays with cotton reels or yogurt pots.

dry with sugar

Use 2 oz of sugar per pound of fruit, 5 g per ½ kg (more can be used according to taste, or added on thawing) and mix gently and then leave in a covered bowl for about 2 hours. The sugar draws moisture from the fruit to produce a coating of syrup. If the fruit has been washed it should not be dried before mixing with sugar: the moisture helps to speed up the process or if the fruit is dry, sprinkle a tablespoonful of cold water on the fruit before mixing with the sugar. Put the sugared fruit into plastic containers for freezing, or open-freeze. A type of crystalisation may form, but generally disappears on thawing; it is not mould and is quite harmless.

This 'dry sugar' method of preparing and freezing is not suitable for apples, apricots, pears and peaches which would be liable to discolour.

in a syrup

Syrup helps to prevent oxidation and discolouring by forming a barrier between fruit and air. To make the syrup, bring the water to the boil and add the sugar, stir it to dissolve properly, then return the sugary liquid to the boil and boil for about two minutes. Let it cool, or chill it, before adding the fruit.

Syrup can be made in various strengths, according to the amount of sugar added to the water.

strength	sugar to add to 1 pint water (500 ml)	enough for how much fruit
weak	4 oz (100 g)	$2\frac{1}{4}$ lb (0·8 kg)
medium	12 oz (300 g)	$2\frac{3}{4}$ lb (1·0 kg)
heavy	16 oz (400 g)	3 lb (1·1 kg)
very heavy	30 oz (750 g)	4 lb (2·5 kg)

purée

Slice the fruit or purée it in a blender with a little water or with diluted lemon juice (in proportion 1 lemon to $1\frac{1}{2}$ pints water) to help prevent discolouration; can be sweetened with sugar or honey; sieve. Freeze in rigid containers, leaving head-space.

preparation

Most kinds of fruit do not need blanching but thin-skinned, delicate fruit, such as apples and pears which brown easily, can be blanched to improve their appearance.

Peach skins are easier to remove if they are immersed briefly in boiling water (and cooled at once in cold water).

Adding ascorbic acid (vitamin C) or citric acid, obtainable from the chemist, can help prevent discolouration. Ascorbic acid can be bought in crystalised form or in tablets of various concentrations. One level teaspoon of crystalised ascorbic acid is sufficient for 6 lb of fruit or for 3 pints of syrup. For smaller quantities of fruit, it is more suitable to use the tablets: three 100 mg tablets of ascorbic acid in ⅓ pint of water or syrup will cover about 10 oz of fruit. Crush the tablets and dissolve them in a little liquid before adding to the main amount of water.

Fruit which is going to be eaten stewed will take up less storage space in the freezer if it is cooked before freezing. It should be sweetened before freezing and should be slightly undercooked to allow for softening when thawing. If soft fruit is going to be used for jam making, sugar (up to about 20% of the weight of the fruit) should be added before freezing. But make a note of this on the label. Do not add sugar to blackcurrants or plums because that would make the skins tough.

Stone fruit can be frozen either with or without the stones. Stoned fruit is liable to collapse when thawed, but is more versatile to use and thaws more quickly than fruit with the stones left in. Cherries for tarts and for garnishes should have the stones left in. If you want to serve up the tart without any stones in, you can take them out when the cherries are half-thawed – this is easier than stoning fresh cherries, and less juice is lost.

storage and thawing

The storage life of most fruit is 12 months. Fruit that has been frozen without sugar keeps less long, so should be used first.

Frozen fruit that will be cooked should be put into a saucepan with a tablespoonful of water and heated gently at first; the heat can be turned up once the juice has begun to run. If syrup-packed fruit or stewed fruit is to be cooked, it does not need the extra water but take care to heat very gently.

Fruit that will be eaten rather than used to make up another dish should be thawed for 4–6 hours in a refrigerator; it will then still be slightly chilled but ready for eating.

Although rapid thawing helps to prevent discolouration, it is better to thaw as slowly as possible (in a refrigerator) because quick thawing will spoil the texture.

fruit

fruit	suitable for freezing	preparation for freezing	notes
apples	**	baked: cook less long than normally, cool before open-freezing; complete the baking on reheating	
		sliced: peel, core and cut into even slices, blanch for 1–2 minutes; pack in a little weak syrup	can also be dry sugar packed or puréed
apricots	**	can be open-frozen whole, but better halved, stoned and put in heavy syrup with some ascorbic acid	very ripe fruit can be puréed, but will keep less long, about 4 months
avocado pears	–	remove stone, can be frozen as halves or slices but better as purée	discolours very quickly. Generally does not freeze well, purée is more successful
bananas	–	purée with sugar and lemon juice	does not freeze well as whole fruit discolours rapidly; thaw in unopened container and use quickly after thawing
blackberries	***	remove stems and leaves, wash and drain; freeze in medium to heavy syrup or in dry sugar pack with a lot of sugar	can be puréed after stewing gently
black currants	***	open-freeze (easier to top and tail when frozen) or stew in minimum amount of water with or without sugar, or dry sugar pack	for later jam-making, blanch for 1 minute before freezing
blueberries	***	open-freeze or pack in medium syrup or dry sugar pack	
cherries	***	wash, remove stalks; can be open-frozen, but better in medium syrup without stones	use ripe red or black cherries; let the juice which runs out when stoning drip into the syrup to conserve the flavour
cranberries	***	can be open-frozen, or purée and make into sauce, then freeze	cook from frozen

notes for gardeners

plant 1 to 3 year old trees in November/March, stake and tie as necessary – crops 4th or 5th year, then for life-time. Trees vary in height from 6 ft (dwarf) to 22 ft. Harvest before fruit fully ripe, when come away from branch with gentle pull.
Grenadier (good pollinator for *Bramley's Seedling*), season August to September; *Lane's Prince Albert*, season January to March; *Bramley's Seedling* (very hardy, not suited to small gardens), season November to March

plant 2 to 3 year old trees, dwarf for small gardens (self-compatible); cropping begins in 4th year; fan-train against south or west facing wall in cool area, or as bush tree, in warmer areas; *Moorpark* (fruit ripens late August)

not cultivated in UK – shop bought

not cultivated in UK – shop bought

rambling cane, plant rooted tips November–March and train; crops on young growth each year; for freezing, harvest just before ripe – August/September; *Bedford Giant, Himalaya Giant* (but not suitable for small gardens)
or use large wild fruit

plant 2 year old certified bushes in November–March, 15 years life; forgo crop first year; fruit in subsequent years on wood produced previous summer; harvest when fully ripe, but before currants fall or shrivel – July/August; *Boskoop Giant* – ripens early but not suitable for small gardens; *Baldwin* – suitable small gardens (rich in vitamin C); *Seabrook's Black; Wellington XXX; Westwick Choice; Malling Jet; Ben Lomond*

plant 2 to 3 year old high-bush variety in autumn or spring on acid soil; five months frost-free season needed; for maximum crop, plant 2 varieties together; harvest when fruit blue/black August to October; *Jersey* (dual-purpose bush for shrub border); *Bluecrop* (fast-growing)

sweet and Duke (not suitable for small garden) plant 1 year old November to March, train as fans on high wall or stake standards and bushes in open. Check compatibility for pollination. Fruits 4th year. Acid – can be grown in small garden; plant 2 to 3 year old tree November to March, fruits 3rd/4th year; fan-train on wall or bush in open. Harvest sweet in May; Duke May to August; acid July/August; leave cherries on tree till ripe and pick with stalks on. *Governor Wood* (self-incompatible) and any dark red; *Morello* (self-compatible acid)

grows wild, but not cultivated in UK; varieties available in USA to grow on naturally moist acid soil

fruit

fruit	suitable for freezing	preparation for freezing	notes
damsons	*	wash, cut in half to remove stones, sweeten purée	freezes better as purée (skins liable to become tough); leaving stones in can alter flavour if stored longer than about 6 months
dates	*	rewrap block dates, remove stones from dessert dates	dates stored in boxes can develop off flavours
figs (fresh)	**	wash in chilled water, remove stems with sharp knife. Peel, slice if required; freeze whole if unpeeled, in light syrup if peeled	handle carefully to avoid bruising
gooseberries	**	wash, top and tail and dry – open-freeze or stew in minimum amount of water – sweetened or unsweetened, or purée or medium syrup	saves storage room to stew or purée before freezing; if for later jelly-making, no need to top and tail
grapefruit	***	peel, remove all pith, skin, pips; pack segments with sugar or in heavy syrup	juice can be frozen sweetened or unsweetened in rigid containers
grapes	*	open-freeze seedless varieties others should be skinned, halved and pipped; light syrup	for decorative purposes a whole bunch may be frozen in a polythene bag and stored for up to 2 weeks
greengages	**	wash, cut in half and remove stones; medium syrup	skins can get tough and stones can flavour fruit
guava	**	cook with a little water and purée or cook and cover with light syrup	cooking in pineapple juice improves flavour
kumquats	**	wrap whole fruit in foil or cover with light syrup	if not in syrup, storage life 2 months
lemons	***	whole fruit can be open-frozen; or cut into slices, separate by film and wrap in polythene	frozen slices can be dropped into drinks or used as garnish; rind of clean lemon grated and stored in small containers keeps six months; juice can be frozen in ice-cube trays and stored in polythene bags

notes for gardeners

---

plant (2 to 3 year old, partly trained by nursery) November–March; stake or support. Fairly hardy, small compact tree – 10/20 ft height and spread; can be grown as bush standard or pyramid. Self-compatible; cropping starts 3rd–6th year; never prune in winter (silver leaf disease); fruits do not ripen simultaneously, 2–3 pickings, start harvest September/October when fruit blue black. *Merryweather; Shropshire Prune*

---

not cultivated in UK – shop bought

---

plant 2 or 3 year old tree November–March; restrict roots with bricks or concrete; as fan against sunny wall; as bush in small garden; half/standard in large garden, stake as necessary. Protect embryo figs in winter, grow in greenhouse where very hard winters. Two crops can be harvested in greenhouse if heated. Harvest when fruit very soft and hangs downwards. No varieties specifically for freezing. *Brown Turkey* open or greenhouse; *White Marseilles* (hardy) harvest August to September; *Bourjasotte Grise* (in greenhouse)

---

plant 1 to 3 year old November–March as bush, cordon or fan. Crops after 3 years for 12 years. Fruits on spurs on older wood and previous summer's lateral growth – self-fertile; protect against birds; thin out large fruits in May; for freezing, harvest when still green June–August. *Careless; Leveller; Whinham's Industry* (red)

---

not normally cultivated in UK – shop bought

---

plant 1 year old grape vine October–March, needs sun, shelter, support against wall on wires, or on wires in open; black varieties need more warmth; *Guyot* crops 3rd year onwards; harvest, depending on variety late August to October; do not handle as spoils bloom

---

plant maiden or 2 to 3 year old tree, south or west facing wall November–March; stake or support fans; cropping 3rd to 6th year; harvest August; never prune in winter (silver leaf disease); no specific varieties for freezing

---

not cultivated in UK – shop bought

---

not cultivated in UK – shop bought

---

not normally cultivated in UK – shop bought

fruit

fruit	suitable for freezing	preparation for freezing	notes
loganberries	***	open-freeze; or dry sugar pack or heavy syrup or purée	
mandarines	**	peel and remove all pith, dry sugar pack or light syrup	
mangoes	**	peel and slice; heavy syrup	add lemon juice to syrup (1 dessertspoonful per pint)
melon	*	cut flesh into cubes or scoops; medium syrup	loses some of its crispness and flavour; serve while still slightly frozen
nectarine	**	peel and stone; light syrup	add lemon juice or ascorbic acid to syrup to prevent discolouration serve while still frosty
oranges	**	peel and remove all pith, dry sugar pack; or light syrup made with orange juice	can also be open-frozen whole, useful during the short seville season, for making marmalade later
peaches	**	remove skin by dipping into boiling water for ½ minute then cool at once in cold; cut in half or slice, remove stone; heavy syrup	prepare syrup first and work quickly as peaches discolour easily; add lemon juice or ascorbic acid
pears	*	skin, core, halve or slice; blanch 1 minute or poach in light syrup then freeze in it	pears lose flavour and texture when frozen raw; freeze cooked pears when nearly tender; thawing completes the softening
pineapple	***	peel, remove eyes, core and cut into slices or dice; heavy syrup	any juice that escapes in preparation should be added to the syrup to conserve the flavour
plums	**	can be open-frozen whole, but better to halve and stone, light syrup or purée	skins toughen and stones flavour flesh if stored for more than 3 months

notes for gardeners

hybrid berry, cultivation as for blackberries; better in full sun and more suited to small gardens; best grown as fan. Pick all fruit when ripe (dark red) – July/August as encourages later fruit to grow fully
Loganberry (thornless)

not normally cultivated in UK – shop bought

not cultivated in UK – shop bought

can be cultivated in cold frames or in greenhouse; cantaloupe (cold frame); musk and winter (greenhouse); harvest June greenhouse, July/October cold frame. No specific varieties for freezing

smooth-skinned mutant of peach, can be grown on south-facing wall in England; plant tree with 5 to 12 shoots November–March as fan; crops 4th year onwards, on shoots made previous summer; do not prune in winter (silver leaf disease and bacterial canker). Start thinning when fruits pea-size, stop when walnut-size; harvest when reddish flush and stalk-end flesh soft: fruit should come away from branch easily – hold fruit in palm of hand, lift and twist; end July–September; no specific varieties for freezing

not normally cultivated in UK – shop bought

as nectarines, but thin out more; harvest mid-July–September; *Hales Early*

plant 1–3 year old trees in November–March, stake and tie; crops 4–5th year onward; trees from 8 ft to 10 ft high. Fruits late June; harvest when slightly under-ripe, when come away from branch with gentle pressure, September–October; no specific varieties for freezing

not cultivated in UK – shop bought

similar to damsons and greengages; plant maiden or 2 or 3 year old nursery-trained tree November–March (dessert plum tree in sun, culinary tolerate some shade). Trees 15–30 ft high; crops 3rd to 6th year. Never prune in winter (silver leaf disease); harvest when fully ripe August–September. No specific variety for freezing

fruit

fruit	suitable for freezing	preparation for freezing	notes
raisins	–	keep well without freezing	
raspberries	***	remove hulls and hard berries, do not wash; open-freeze or in dry sugar pack	purée damaged berries
red currants	***	as black currants	
rhubarb	***	wash, trim, cut into 2 in pieces, blanch for 1 minute; pack with or without sugar or light syrup	to freeze cooked, put in casserole with brown sugar or golden syrup no added water and cook till tender; pack in rigid containers with crumpled film between contents and lid
strawberries	***	open-freeze or pack with sugar or in heavy syrup, or purée	open-frozen strawberries tend to go flabby if thoroughly thawed
sultanas	–	keep well without freezing	
white currants	***	as for black currants	

plant canes November–March (government inspected, certified stock virus-free, healthy and true to name), plants should last 10 years, then choose new site. Train canes on wires in rows; fair crop in 2nd year, full subsequently.
Summer-fruiting type fruits on laterals from previous year's canes; protect from birds with netting pick fruit without stalk and core June–September; after harvest, cut down fruited canes to ground level and tie in new ones.
Autumn-fruiting types fruit on top part of current season's canes; harvest September till frosts; cut down all canes in February, new canes produced in spring.
Lloyd George, Glen Cova, early summer, best planted on own as susceptible to virus infection; *Norfolk Giant, September,* autumn fruiting, ripen late August–early September

certified stock not available; plant 1 or 2 year old bush or 2 to 3 year old cordon to train up vertical cane. Protect blossoms, buds and fruit against frost and birds with netting; plants crop for 10 years; crops on permanent framework in clusters at base of 1 year old shoots, and on short spurs on older wood; harvest July–August, pick whole clusters to avoid injury to fruit. No specific varieties for freezing

prepare bed in autumn before planting; plant sets cut from 3 year old plants (ensure each has at least one bud) in October to November or February to March on sunny site, but will tolerate most conditions. Forgo crop first year and pull lightly second, always leave 3 to 4 leaves on each plant to avoid weakening. Harvest March–May when stalks pink and tender, before leaves fully open; leaves poisonous; hold stick near base and twist and pull, do not cut (encourages rot). Earlier crop possible January–February by forcing.
Victoria

if space limited grow in pots, growbags but yield less. *Summer-fruiting* crops once in early summer, *perpetual* crops irregularly throughout summer till stopped by frost; *alpine* mountain form of wild, crops continuously or in flushes June–November.
Plant *summer fruiting* virus-free stock in July/August; if later than mid-September forgo maiden crop; prepare bed well because in use 3/4 years; when fruit swelling, put down straw; protect from birds; can also grow through black polythene; harvest June–August, complete with stalks, flesh bruises easily so try not to handle. After cropping, cut off old leaves and unwanted runners, clear away and burn straw; propagate from runners. *Cambridge Favourite, Cambridge Vigour, Totem* (freeze well), *Redgauntlet, Royal Sovereign*
plant *perpetual* in summer, autumn, spring; size of crop deteriorates in second year: replant with new runners each year; treat as for summer fruiting, otherwise dig up plants after fruiting; no specific variety for freezing
Alpine grow from seed in autumn and overwinter in cold frame, or sow in March under glass, plant out seedlings in May in open or light shade; harvest June–November; small prolific fruits, can propagate from runners but difficult to maintain virus-free stock, re-sow after 2 years. No specific varieties for freezing

dried fruit

as for red currants; no specific varieties for freezing

Vegetables

Some vegetables can be easily bought at low prices, all the year round. So – particularly when freezer space is limited – it makes more sense to freeze expensive vegetables which have a short season, or vegetables of which there is a sudden glut.

It is not economical to use freezer space for vegetables that store well by other means (most root vegetables keep well even in the ground). But baby carrots and turnips may be worth freezing or make up a mixed bag of prepared root vegetables, blanch each type separately, cool, mix and pack in small quantities for soups or stews or sauces.

– no frozen salads

Frozen and-then-thawed vegetables lose their crispness and are therefore better used cooked than raw. So, if all your lettuces are ready at the same time, cook some for a few minutes before freezing and serve instead of cabbage – it is more tender; try a sprinkling of caraway seed to make it definitely different.

blanching

Enzymes, which are chemical elements responsible for the processes of ripening and development of vegetables, spoil the vegetables if allowed to be over-active. Blanching inactivates the enzymes, preventing discolouration and changes in texture, and loss of aroma and flavour, during the frozen state.

Blanching involves subjecting the vegetables to boiling water for a specified time and then plunging them into iced water to cool quickly.

how to blanch

- half fill your largest saucepan (or pressure cooker, if you have one) with water
- bring to the boil
- use a wire basket (eg from the chip pan) or a muslin bag, or a blanching basket (sold in freezer shops)
- put the vegetables into the (pre-heated) basket and immerse in boiling water
- bring the water back to the boil quickly (put a lid on the saucepan if it fits with the basket)
- measure the blanching time from the moment the water returns to the boil
- after the blanching time has elapsed, quickly lift out the basket and cool the vegetables for about the same length of time as the blanching
- drain thoroughly (in a colander) then turn onto absorbent paper.

Prepare the vegetables (peel, cut, trim) before blanching. Process only a few vegetables at a time. The water should return to the boil within a minute of adding the vegetables. If it takes longer than this, the amount processed each time should be reduced. The blanching time depends on the size and type of vegetable; do not blanch for longer than necessary. If a range of blanching times is given, the shorter is for small or young vegetables. The aim of blanching is to stop enzyme activity, not to cook the vegetables. Cooling quickly is important as otherwise the vegetables will continue to cook in their own heat. A large bowl of water with icecubes is ideal for the purpose.

Processing a large quantity of vegetables requires a remarkable quantity of icecubes, since chilling should take no more time than the blanching. The domestic refrigerator is unlikely to be able to supply enough, so collect a number of yogurt pots, put them on to a baking tray, fill with water and freeze. The resulting blocks pop out quite easily and can be packed in polythene bags and stored in any available space in the freezer. No need to break them up before use.

While the cooling water must be changed frequently, there is no need to boil fresh blanching water for each batch; it can be used about 7 times and may even improve the vitamin C retention.

To blanch large quantities of vegetables, use double the equipment: two large saucepans and two bowls of iced water. While the first lot of vegetables is cooling and the first saucepan is re-boiling, use the second saucepan and cool in the second bowl, and vice versa. A definite rhythm can be established and all the vegetables are processed in a much shorter time.

is it necessary to blanch?

It must be a dedicated cook who never questions whether it is worth all the effort required in blanching. Sometimes it can be dispensed with. For example, unblanched peas can be kept for 6–9 months and small carrots about 12 months. But storage times are usually drastically reduced: unblanched broad beans develop 'off' flavours in about 3 weeks and corn on the cob and runner beans after about 4 weeks. If you freeze vegetables unblanched, label them as unblanched and use them before any you have blanched.

packaging

Vegetables can be packed immediately in bags or boxes. But it is often better to open-freeze, that is, to freeze the vegetables in individual pieces spread out on a baking tray. Once frozen, they should be packed in boxes or bags. The advantage of this method is that they do not get stuck together during freezing and as much or as little as is wanted can be removed from the freezer.

storing

Most vegetables have a storage life of 12 months but the more water they contain, the shorter the storage time on the whole – and the more is their texture affected when thawed.

growing vegetables for freezing

People whose garden is not big enough to grow a lot of fruit and vegetables should give some thought to their planting, so as to make the most of their freezer.

It is worth growing vegetables that have a short season and lengthening their availability by freezing. Sweetcorn, for example, is a crop that is at its best for only a short time and freezing lengthens the availability.

Or grow for freezing vegetables that are susceptible to attack by pests or disease at certain times of the year. Cauliflower, for example, suffers from caterpillar and club root, so that people find it a difficult crop to grow well in the summer without spending much time and money on pest and disease control. By growing early summer cauliflower, these pests and diseases can be made less of a problem and freezing gives a supply for the rest of the year.

By growing early crops of peas and harvesting broad beans young, the area they are grown on can be used for other crops later on. Also the early crops require minimal staking and tend to yield better than later crops. This helps to give more cropping on the same area of land.

There would seem little point in freezing a crop if it can be produced fresh all the year round. However, in the winter, many people can get into their garden only during the hours of darkness or at weekends and might prefer to have the majority of their vegetables frozen by late autumn so that they can get them from the freezer, rather than having to take a torch into the garden.

Bear in mind that most vegetables intended for freezing should usually be harvested a little earlier than vegetables which are to be used straightaway. It is only worth freezing vegetables of the highest quality, when they are young and tender.

Vegetables for freezing should be picked at their prime: do not delay picking until the peak is past, or decide to eat the best and freeze the rest, but rather freeze the best and eat the rest.

Summer holidays can sometimes be a stumbling block to harvesting crops when they are at their best. The crops most affected are those requiring regular harvesting to keep the produce young and tender, such as runner beans, french beans, courgettes, peas. By sowing runner beans, sweetcorn and courgettes late, harvesting need not begin until after the August holidays; with crops such as peas or cauliflower, harvesting can be before the holidays.

Most seed catalogues from the main seed merchants indicate varieties specially suitable for freezing. They are generally chosen for their uniformity of size and growth (that is, being ready to harvest at the same time), such as F1 hybrids.

To help make the best use of the soil many crops can be sown in trays or pots and transplanted (but not, for example, carrots or parsnips). Any container can be used, including egg cartons, but it should be clean and there must always be drainage. Plant out before the seedlings receive a check. If weather conditions are unfavourable when planting is due, and the task has to be postponed, be prepared to liquid-feed. Saturate the soil with water immediately before planting.

By transplanting, extra time is gained, either for the crop in the ground or for the crop that is to follow – or maybe both. The extra week or fourteen days gained can make all the difference between one and two crops being harvested from a given area in a year. Normally a more uniform crop can be grown which makes it easier to harvest in one or two pickings and that makes freezing easier.

vegetables

vegetable		preparation for freezing, and use after thawing	blanching time, min	notes for gardeners
asparagus	**	scrape, cut off wooden parts of stems, pack in boxes to protect heads; cook from frozen as usual	2–4	buy one-year old crowns for planting in April; plants last about 20 years, but do not produce till year 3 or 4. Freezer storage life up to 9 months
artichokes	**	take off outer leaves and trim base; cook from frozen in lots of salted water	7–10	grown from suckers taken from base of established plants March–April; 3-year crop, plants at best when two years old
aubergines	**	cut in half lengthwise or into slices; can be frozen whole for later stuffing	5	grow in greenhouse or under cloche in sunny sheltered part of garden; harvesting late August–September when they are rich purple
beans, broad	***	shell; discard any very large ones; cook in salted boiling water for 8 min	3	two sowing times: October/November for overwintering (pick June) *Aquadulce*, or March onwards to pick July onwards: *Masterpiece Green Longpod, The Sutton*
beans, french	***	string, if necessary; trim off ends, cut into pieces if required; cook in salted boiling water for 5 min (cut) or 7 min (whole)	if cut 2 if whole 3	two varieties, dwarf and climbing; dwarf sow from May to July successively, *Masterpiece, Tendergreen, The Prince,* regular picking ensures continuous supply; for climbing, erect supports before sowing or planting to avoid damaging roots, sow early May *Blue Lake, Purple Podded*; pick July

vegetable		preparation for freezing, and use after thawing	blanching time, min	notes for gardeners
beans, runner	***	string and trim off ends, slice, do not shred too finely or cooked result will be tasteless; for thin slices, cut after blanching; cook in salted boiling water for 7 min	2	sow early May onwards, pick August onwards, *Kelvedon Marvel, Streamline, Scarlet Emperor*; regular picking, in height of season every other day, encourages more crop
beetroot	**	only small ones suitable for freezer; cook for 25-30 min or until tender, cool quickly; can be frozen whole; larger ones should be diced; store only 6 months; thaw in refrigerator for 2 hours	nil (cooked)	early crop March/April, main crop May/June; useful for intercropping or catch crop; takes 12 weeks to mature; lift all by November; *Crimson Globe, Detroit Little Ball*
broccoli	***	remove woody stems and outer leaves; cook from frozen in salted boiling water for 8 min	small 3 med 4 thick 5	hardy; will grow where cauliflower will not; sow in tray or seedbed mid April/May, transplant June/July, will mature the following year from January to May; *White Sprouting* (better flavour) February to March, *Purple Sprouting* (very hardy)
brussels sprouts	***	remove outer leaves, use small buttons, cut cross into base; cook from frozen in salted boiling water for 8 min	3	sow in prepared seedbed end March, transplant late May/June, harvest mid-October to late December, gather buttons from bottom of stem upwards when still tight; with conventional varieties sprouts mature a few at a time; F1 hybrids *Citadel, Peer Gynt* more uniform
cabbage	**	not worth freezing, available all year round		

calabrese	***	use only tender sprigs, cut to suitable lengths; pack in rigid container to protect heads; cook from frozen in salted boiling water for 8 min	3	sow in seedbed or small pots April/May, transplant June/July after other earlier crops; if dry irrigate; 12–14 weeks to maturity; smaller spears freeze better, so plant close; remove central head from plant to allow side shoots to develop; pick them every few days when 4 in long; *Express Corona, Green Comet*
carrots	***	trim, slice, dice or leave whole as desired; peel after blanching; cook from frozen in salted boiling water for 8 min	whole 5 sliced or diced 3	early (short) variety (eg *Amsterdam Forcing*) sow March, mature from June; main crop (intermediate *Chantenay Red Cored* and long *Saint Valery*) plant June, mature from August; beware carrot fly: pull early, rotation with other crops helps
cauliflower	**	trim and separate into florets, soak in salt water (1 tsp to 2 pints of water) cook from frozen in salted boiling water for 10 min leftover stalks: boil or steam and pass through blender, freeze, use as basis of soup	3	sow summer variety (*Dominant*) in January in gentle warmth, plant out March; or sow September, prick out into frames to overwinter and plant out March; harvest when heads firm (do not let curds open out) from June. *Predominant* (summer) seed or seedlings planted very close produce high yield of mini-cauliflower suitable for freezing whole
celeriac	**	peel, cut into slices or boil till almost cooked then peel; cook from frozen or thaw 2–5 hours in salad dressing or puree before freezing and thaw gently	3–4	sow mid-March in seedbox; in cold greenhouse, frame or under cloche in April; plant out late May/early June after hardening off; water well during growing; harvest October or in mild area leave in ground protected with straw against frost; *Globus*

vegetable		preparation for freezing, and use after thawing	blanching time, min	notes for gardeners
celery	**	remove ends and any strings, wash well, cut into pieces cook from frozen in salted boiling water for 5 min or add to stew etc, not for salads or eating raw	3	sow in seedbox March/April, plant out late May/early June in trench in double staggered rows (trench method of growing prevents feathery leaf spot) water well during growing; earth up at 3 week intervals, preferably after rain, to cover leaf bases and therefore blanch stems; harvest October-February, lift carefully with trowel or fork; cover trench with bracken or straw in frosty weather to help lifting no specific variety for freezing
chicory	**	steam from frozen or braise with butter, or bake; not for eating raw	2	not worth growing especially for freezing
chinese leaves	–	does not freeze well: crispness is lost		
courgettes	**	wipe clean, trim ends, do not peel; freeze whole, halved or in thick slices cook from frozen in salted boiling water for 3 min or thaw and saute in butter or open-freeze in thin slices and dip frozen in batter and fry	whole 2-3 sliced 1½	sow in pots mid-March for early crop, plant out through black polythene under cloches early May; sow mid-April for planting out early June; direct sow early/mid-May into holes in prepared mounds when danger of frost past; harvest when 4 to 6 in long, regular cutting ensures further cropping; *Early Gem*
cucumber	–	does not freeze well		

fennel	**	3–4	trim and wash well, chop or slice pack in rigid containers cover with (blanching) liquid; 6 months storage; simmer from frozen in blanching liquid or stock for 30 min; for salads, thaw in salad dressing	sow April-July in greenhouse and transplant 4 weeks later; can be sown directly outside April onwards; when plant base swells to golf ball size, earth up soil for 4 weeks to blanch leaf base, or blanch using cardboard collar; harvest 4 weeks after start of blanching late June-late September; cut beneath basal stems when tennis ball size; no specific variety for freezing
kale	***	3	remove from stems, wash, discard dry or tough leaves, chop; 6 months' storage; cook from frozen in boiling water for 8 min	very hardy; sow April/May in prepared seedbed, transplant late June/early August; sow rape varieties in May, leave in final growing position; earth up to base of first leaves to protect against frost and wind; harvest November–April after other brassica crops, best after frost; use young leaves and shoots only; pick side shoots from top downwards
leeks	**	3–4	remove outer leaves, trim ends, slit to wash well 6 months' storage; cook from frozen in boiling water for 7–10 min	early variety sow in greenhouse late January-early February, plant late April; main variety sow in seedbed outside March–April; plant May/June; late variety sow June plant July (crops next spring); plant in 6 in deep holes when 6–8 in high or in 2 in deep trench; long stems/blanching obtained by earthing up; no specific variety for freezing
lettuce	–		does not freeze well; becomes limp	

vegetable		preparation for freezing, and use after thawing	blanching time min	notes for gardeners
marrow	**	peel and remove seeds, slice; cook from frozen in boiling water for 4 min; old ones, wash and cook before freezing; gently reheat (stuffed marrow can also be frozen) 6 months' storage	3	sow in mid-April in pots, plant out at one true leaf early June; or direct sow May when all danger of frost past into tops of prepared mounds. Stop laterals of trailing varieties at 24 in; harvest July/September, cut all in September before frost; no specific variety for freezing
mushrooms	*	trim and slice if desired, rinse, freeze while damp or sauté in butter for 5 min before freezing (with the butter from sauté) 3 months' storage thaw in refrigerator then add to dishes as required; or warm gently under grill or in oven	nil	extremely difficult for 'home gardeners' to produce; reliably uniform compost needed; proprietory bags, boxes and tubs of spawned mushroom compost can be bought
onions	**	peel and chop large ones; freeze small pickling ones whole; overwrap to prevent cross-flavouring; 6 months' storage; add to soups and stews while still frozen, or sauté as raw; serve while still frosty in salads	2–3	not worth growing for freezer (not really worth freezing) because store so well dry
parsnips	**	freeze young ones; trim, peel and slice; cook from frozen in boiling water for 10 min, or bake	2	keeps well in ground or stored in sand therefore not worth growing for freezing

peas	***	pod, blanch in small quantities to ensure even heat distribution cook from frozen in boiling salted water for 5 min	1	sow first earlies January/February, protect with cloches, harvest June; successive sowings March–end April, harvest from mid-June–August, further sowings till end June, harvest till September. Protect seeds and seedlings from birds with fine-mesh wire netting, support when 3–4 in tall with netting or twigs for plants to climb; pick regularly (4 weeks after full flower) to encourage development of more pods, pick from base first; beware pea moth. First early: *Feltham First, Kelvedon Wonder,* (mildew resisting), *Early Onward, Dark Skinned Perfection;* second early: *Hurst Green Shaft, Onward* (hardy)
peas mange-tout	***	freeze when young (flat) wash, remove ends and any strings; cook from frozen in boiling salted water for 7 min	2	sow and cultivate as garden peas; mange-touts reach 4 ft height, pods are edible but important that peas inside have not started to swell and only young ones harvested (harvest as for garden peas); *Oregon Sugar Pod*
peppers green or red	***	wash, remove all seeds and stem, halve or slice add frozen to dishes as required	3 (colour affected by blanching)	require protection to do well; sow in seedbox, transplant singly into small pots, plant out in greenhouse, border soil, growbags or large pots; or outside mid-June protected with cloches; harvest July onward greenhouse, late August/September outdoors. Normally harvested green; most varieties turn red when left on plant. *Canape, Bullnose Ace*

vegetable	preparation for freezing, and use after thawing	blanching time, min	notes for gardeners
potatoes	on the whole potatoes do not freeze well	–	not worth growing for freezing; dry store
pumpkin	peel and remove seeds, chop or purée; 6 months' storage; cook from frozen in boiling salted water for 3 min, thaw puree in refrigerator for 2 hours, heat with butter in double boiler or use in pie	* 3	sow and cultivate as courgettes; keep pumpkins off ground in September; harvest September before frost, store in nets or shelves in dry frost-free place; no specific variety for freezing – not worth cultivating for freezing
radishes	do not freeze well, become limp	–	
spinach	strip off stems, wash thoroughly, cook without extra water; saves space to freeze cooked (whole or chopped) heat from frozen for 2–3 min in a little top of milk or butter	*** not worth blanching freeze cooked	sow March–May at 2/3 week intervals, thin to 6 in apart; harvest 8–10 weeks after sowing; sow winter spinach late August/ September on sunny site, protect with cloches from October; 12 weeks to mature; pick only few leaves at a time, outside leaves when young and tender to encourage further cropping. Very fast growing, can be grown as catch crop between rows of taller vegetables eg beans or peas. *New Zealand* good for freezing, milder flavour than ordinary spinach; soak seeds overnight before sowing indoors in early March, plant out May or when no more frost danger, thin seedlings; trailing habit: takes up lot of ground but does not bolt; pinch out tips of well grown plants to produce more branching and young leaves; harvest June–September
swedes	trim, peel and dice cook from frozen in boiling salted water for 8–10 min or cook and puree before freezing	*** 2–3	not worth growing for freezing, keeps in ground till following spring

sweetcorn	***	trim, remove husk and silk, wash, scrape off kernels and open-freeze or freeze whole; thaw cobs 1 hr at room temp or put frozen into cold unsalted water, boil for 15 min; kernels 5 min	small 4 med 6 large 8 (keeps 4 weeks unblanched)	unless large growing area available, keep to one variety; sow pre-germinated seeds in small containers in greenhouse in April; plant late May as soon as seedlings are 1½ in high, not in row but in block 12–18 in apart (to allow wind pollination); in northern areas protect in frames or cloches until early June. Harvest when silks darkened and kernels a pale yellow full of creamy (not watery) liquid when thumbnail-tested: gently ease back protective sheaf round kernels to test; if not ready, replace sheaf or sparrows will eat the corn. Remove cob by snapping downwards. *Earliking; Kelvedon Glory*
tomatoes	**	remove skin by plunging into boiling water for 30 secs, or purée firm ripe small ones can be frozen whole to add to dishes or grill, not suitable for use in salads	nil	sow in March, prick off into individual pots keeping frost-free; plant out under cloches early May or in open after frost danger past. Stop standard varieties by end July (usually 4–5 trusses) bush types (*Sleaford Abundance, Alfresco*) are better planted through black polythene to keep fruit clean and weeds controlled. For earlier crop grow in greenhouse (sow January to March) directly in border soil, or if pest or diesease problem, ring culture, strawbales, large compost filled pots, or growbags; harvest May to November; *Gardeners Delight* small standard cherry variety
turnips	***	trim, peel, dice or leave small ones whole, or purée; cook from frozen in boiling salted water for 8–10 min, reheat purée gently	whole 4 diced 2	not worth growing for freezing
watercress	–	does not freeze satisfactorily		

Freezing roses

A freezer does not have to be used exclusively for storing food. This summer, try freezing roses. Choose good quality blooms just before they begin to open. They can be frozen simply by laying on a tray until frozen and then wrapped well. Or, alternatively, lay them in a container, fill with water and freeze. Frozen flowers are very delicate and can easily be damaged so the latter method is preferable – but it does take up a lot of room.

Thaw gently, and put into water – a lovely display for the Christmas table. Roses freeze well, but you could experiment with other types of flowers.

Handbuch Tiefgefrieren
on which the idea of this Consumer Publication is based
is published by the German consumer organisations
Arbeitsgemeinschaft der Verbraucher e.V and *Institut
für angewandte Verbraucherforschung e.V.*

Some relevant *Which?* reports

Bread	Nov 1976	Fridge-freezers (cont.)	Jul 1976
Bulk buying	Jun 1977		Oct 1976
– frozen food	Jun 1974		May 1977
– icecream	Jul 1977		Jun 1980
– meat	Jan 1976	Frozen food	Sep 1970
Cheese	Feb 1980	– bulk buying	Jun 1974
Chicken buying and cooking	Dec 1980	Fruit – fresh	Sep 1978
buying hints	Dec 1980	Fruit – buying trees and	
Cold boxes and bags	Apr 1979	bushes	May 1977 [Han]
Discounts		– growing your own	
electrical appliances	May 1980		May 1977 [Han]
Duck buying and cooking	Dec 1980	Gamebirds	Dec 1980
buying hints	Dec 1976	Greenhouses	Aug 1972 [Han]
Electrical appliances:			Aug 1978 [Han]
– reliability and servicing	Feb 1977	Growing bags	Feb 1979 [Han]
– repair services	Jul 1979		Nov 1979 [Han]
Fish fingers – frozen	Apr 1970	House contents insurance	
Food – frozen	Sep 1970		Dec 1981 [Mon]
	Jun 1974	Icecream	Jul 1977
	May 1977	– makers	Jul 1981
– hygiene	Jan 1981	Meat – bulk buying	Jan 1976
– storage	Aug 1975	Microwave ovens	Mar 1975
Freezer contents insurance	Jun 1979		Nov 1979
Freezers		Plant propagators	Feb 1978 [Han]
– large	Sep 1970	– raising	Feb 1978 [Han]
	Dec 1970	Poultry – frozen	Apr 1971
	Apr 1971	Repairs – electrical goods	Jul 1979
	Jan 1975		Jul 1980
	Jul 1975	Seeds and cuttings	
– medium chest	Mar 1978	propagation	Feb 1978 [Han]
– medium upright	Nov 1976	Soil –acid or alkaline	Nov 1976 [Han]
	Aug 1978	– testing kits	Feb 1972 [Han]
– small chest	May 1981	Symbols for storage	Jun 1980
– small chest and upright	Sep 1970	Thermometers – cooking	Sep 1974
– small worktop	Jun 1980	Turkeys – buying and cooking	Dec 1980
Fridge-freezers	Aug 1972	– buying hints	Dec 1976
	Jul 1973	Vegetables – growing own	Feb 1975

Gardening from Which?

A new magazine, designed to help you make the most of your garden, appears ten times a year. It embraces all the main areas of interest to every gardener. Like *Which?* the new *Gardening from Which?* buys goods anonymously, researches and tests them thoroughly and publishes the findings in clear comprehensive reports. There are topical 'bumper' issues at the relevant times of the year.

thermometer
– freezer, 28, 29, 38, 80
– meat, 61, 88
thermostat, 15, 18, 19, 34, 35,
  38, 39, 74
tilting, 11, 34, 67, 78
tomatoes, 58, 131
trout, 98
turbot, 98
turkey, 93,
turnip, 31

upright freezer, 6, 13, 15, 22 *et
  seq*, 38
– advantages, 13, 15
– defrosting, 63
– insulation, 40
– size, 6, 122
– warm spot, 38
use-by date, 40, 45, 65

veal, 90
vegetables, 123 *et seq*
– after power cut, 68
– amounts, 82

– blanching, 29, 57, 58, 123 *et
  seq*
– cooling, 61
– growing for freezing, 121
– notes for gardeners, 123 *et seq*
– varieties for freezing, 123 *et
  seq*
venison, 93
ventilation, 6, 35, 69

warm air, 6, 8, 46
watercress, 131
waxed paper, 52
Which? reports, 27, 31, 133
whitebait, 98
white currants, 116
wine, 53
wire tags, 50
wrapping, 46 *et seq*, 49
woodcock, 93

yeast, 103
yogurt, 105
– pots, 50, 107

Avoiding back trouble

tells you about the spine and what can go wrong with it, concentrating mainly on the lower back. It advises on ways of avoiding back trouble, and for those who suffer from backache already, offers guidance on how to ease it, how to live with it and how to avoid becoming a chronic sufferer. It deals with causes of back trouble, specialist examination and treatment and gives hints on general care of the back when sitting, standing, lifting, carrying, doing housework, gardening, driving.

Avoiding heart trouble

identifies the factors which make a person more likely to develop heart trouble and describes how the various risk factors interact: cigarette smoking, raised blood pressure, high level of blood fats, stress, hereditary and dietary factors, oral contraceptives, overweight. It warns of the more serious signs and symptoms of heart trouble and, where possible, tells you what can be done about them.

Central heating

helps you to choose central heating for your home, giving details of the equipment involved – boilers, radiators, heat emitters, thermostats and other controls, warm air units, ducting – and discussing the different fuels, the importance of insulation, and the installation.

Earning money at home

for the person who has to stay at home and would like to make some money at the same time, the book explains what this entails in the way of organising domestic life, family and children, keeping accounts, taking out insurance, coping with tax, costing, dealing with customers, getting supplies. It suggests many activities that could be undertaken, with or without previous experience.

Living through middle age

faces up to the physical changes and psychological difficulties for both men and women that this stage of life may bring (some inevitable and some avoidable). Throughout, practical advice is given on overcoming problems, so that you can make the most of your middle years.

Extending your house
describes what is involved in having an extension built on to a house
or bungalow, explaining what has to be done, when and by whom. It
explains how the Building Regulations affect the position and design
of an extension, and how to apply for planning permission and Building
Regulations approval.

Getting a new job
is a practical guide to the steps to take from when one job ends to the
day the next one begins. The circumstances relating to unfair dismissal
are explained and the remedies available. The book defines redundancy
and lists your rights, it explains how redundancy payment is calculated
and what can be done when an employer does not pay up. It also
suggests how an employer can help a redundant employee find a job.

The book deals with job hunting, how to apply, what to do to get an
interview and making sure that the interview goes well. The book deals
with the points to consider when being offered a job and what is
involved as an employee – the legal rights and obligations on both
sides.

The legal side of buying a house
covers the procedure for buying an owner-occupied house with a
registered title in England or Wales (not Scotland) and describes the
part played by the solicitors and building society, the estate agent,
surveyor, Land Registry, insurance company and local authority. It
takes the reader step by step through a typical house purchase so that,
in many cases, he can do his own conveyancing without a solicitor; it
also deals with the legal side of selling.

The newborn baby
deals primarily with the first weeks after the baby is born, with information about feeding and development in the following weeks and
months. The daily routines, such as feeding, bathing, nappy changing,
sleeping, are covered and the book tells how to identify and cope with
minor upsets that may cause alarm but are normal and also the more
serious ailments that should be reported to the doctor. The book also
deals with matters such as immunisation, tests, visits to the clinic.

On getting divorced
explains the procedure for getting a divorce in England or Wales, and how, in a straightforward undefended case, it can be done by the postal procedure. The legal advice scheme and other state help for someone with a low income is described and there is advice on coping in reduced circumstances. Calculations for maintenance and division of property are given, with details of the orders the court may make for financial settlements between the divorcing couple and for arrangements about the children.

Raising the money to buy your home
explains the choice of mortgage and lender that faces you when needing a loan to buy your first or a new home. It deals with building societies, banks, local authorities, insurance companies, warning about the limitations and conditions that each may impose. The book describes how interest rates can vary and shows, with tables, the difference between the quoted interest rate and what you actually pay. There are also calculations to enable you to work out your own payments on a repayment mortgage. The book takes you through the steps of applying for a loan, and deals with what happens if you have difficulty with keeping up the payments or want to pay off your mortgage.

Securing your home
should help you keep burglars and car thieves at bay by telling you how to protect your home and safe-guard your car. It gives practical advice on making it difficult for the burglar to get in (locks and grilles, burglar alarms, and general safety are all dealt with). And it tells you what to do and not to do if a burglar has broken into your home or car, and how to make a claim on your insurance.

What to do when someone dies
explains about doctors' certificates, about deaths reported to the coroner and what this entails, about registering a death and getting the various certificates that may be needed afterwards. Differences between burial and cremation procedure are discussed, and the arrangements that have to be made, mainly through the undertaker, for the funeral. The book details the various national insurance benefits that may be claimed.

Where to live after retirement
tackles the difficult subject of a suitable place to live in old age. The book offers practical advice on the decision whether to move or to stay put and adapt the present home to be easier to live in. It weighs up the pros and cons of the alternatives open to an older person, and the financial aspects involved, considers sheltered housing and granny flats, the problems of living in someone else's household, and residential homes.

Which? way to buy, sell and move house
takes you through all the stages of moving to another home – considering the pros and cons of different places, house hunting, viewing, having a survey, making an offer, getting a mortgage, completing the purchase, selling the present home. It explains the legal procedures and the likely costs. Buying and selling at an auction and in Scotland are specifically dealt with. The practical arrangements for the move and for any repairs or improvements to the new house are described. Advice is given for easing the tasks of sorting, packing and moving possessions, people and pets, with a removal firm or by doing it yourself, and for making the day of the move go smoothly.

Which? way to slim
is the complete guide to losing weight and staying slim. The book separates fact from fallacy, and gives a balanced view of essentials such as suitable weight ranges, target weights, exercise, and the advantages and disadvantages of different methods of dieting. The book highlights the dangers of being overweight and warns of the risks in middle age, during pregnancy, when giving up smoking. Every aspect of slimming is appraised – from appetite suppressants to yoga.
There are also sections on slimmers' cookery, foods and aids for slimmers, eating out, slimming groups, help from doctors, the psychology of slimming, activity and exercise. Tables of Calorie and carbohydrate values of foods and drinks are provided for easy day-to-day reference.

CONSUMER PUBLICATIONS are available from Consumers' Association, Caxton Hill, Hertford SG13 7LZ, and from booksellers.